CRASH

TEST

My Brother's Accident
and the Race of Our Lives

CRASH
TEST

CHRIS BYE

FOREWORD BY SCOTT GOODYEAR

BASTIAN
BOOKS

Published by Bastian Books
Toronto, Canada
www.bastianbooks.com
A division of Bastian Publishing Services Ltd.

Distributed by Publishers Group Canada
www.pgcbooks.ca

ISBN 978-0-9780554-9-3

Cataloguing in Publication Data available from Library and Archives Canada

Cover design and typesetting: Daniel Crack, Kinetics Design
www.kdbooks.ca
Cover photograph by Daniel Crack courtesy of AIM Autosport
Text photographs courtesy of Gridwork

Printed and bound in Canada by Webcom

To Cathy and Hailey

CONTENTS

FOREWORD

Some think if you make your living driving race cars, you become numb to the fact that people you know and care about could get hurt – or die – in a racing accident. It seems that way because race-car drivers don't talk about the possibility, and try not to think about it. We all feel it will never happen to us. We're more worried about the commute from event to event than the races themselves.

Once drivers strap themselves into the cockpit of a race car and head out onto the track, danger presents itself in each and every lap. Perhaps at no other place than Indy is the risk higher. With speeds consistently over 230 miles per hour, and with concrete walls as a safety net to keep cars in the park, the Speedway, as it is known around the world, is an unforgiving environment. For drivers and their spouses, sons, daughters, and parents, this is a scary place. Since the first race at the Speedway, in 1911, drivers have had a love–hate relationship with it. History shows that you need to treat this facility with respect. There is a list of both rookies and veterans who didn't.

Screeching tires followed by a loud thump alerts you to the obvious. A strange quiet comes over the racetrack. A silent communication takes place between all who are there. As a driver you sit in the cockpit of your race car on pit lane waiting for the track to return to green. The accident is now compartmentalized somewhere deep in your brain so it doesn't affect the job at hand. You are a professional. You are programmed not to let events like this affect your purpose in life.

I remember the moment I was told about the highway accident of Porsche racer and friend Rick Bye. I remember thinking how strange it was that Rick, whom I had raced against driving powerful Porsche turbo race cars, and at some of the most difficult racetracks in the world, was now fighting for his life after a non-race-related accident. After several thousands of miles on the racetrack at speeds reaching 200 miles per hour, Rick had never even broken a bone in his body, and now he was in danger of not making it out of the emergency room. With this news, it was time to find a quiet place and reflect.

I spent the next several months testing and racing my Indy Car, now more aware of the present danger associated with my profession, and always asking about Rick's condition. This is a road many of us have been down before. Although you hope for good news, in the back of your mind you are prepared for the worst.

Those of us who have succeeded in becoming professional drivers did so by never giving up. Rick would never give up – he would defy all odds. And after flirting with death, Rick was back. I remember being invited to speak at a benefit to help him and his family in my hometown of Toronto. Although this was called a benefit, it really was a celebration of life, Rick was getting something not many people in our profession are given: a second chance.

I realized through this experience, and now through reading *Crash Test*, just how lucky Rick was to survive. Events like Rick's make you realize that life can be fragile, no matter what you do for a living. We are indebted to Rick's brother, Chris, for recounting Rick's accident and recovery in dramatic detail in this exciting and inspiring book, however painful it must have been for him to do so.

There is a lesson here for all of us.

Life may only come around once. Live each day to its fullest.

Scott Goodyear

PREFACE

Writing this book has been the hardest thing I've ever done, second only to sitting by my brother Rick's bed in intensive care after his highway accident on the way to competing in the Rolex 24 Hours at Daytona Sports Car Race. Maybe because this was never meant to be a book. The process started with thousands of words torpedoing around in my head. Every time I tried to get them out, my mouth wouldn't work. And when my mouth did work, the words couldn't get past the lump in my throat. Then late one night I learned that the words could escape from my head through my fingertips.

Random words began to fill my computer screen. At times they came out as slow as molasses. Other times they came out with fury, like bullets from a machine gun. At times I just sat and stared at the computer screen for hours with nothing to add. Other times my fingers moved faster than I ever thought possible, as if possessed. Then the sun would come up.

As time went on I realized that putting these words together was a form of therapy, helping me make sense of the turmoil inside me. I sat and looked at them for hours. And then I started to place them in order. The more order I gave to them, the more sense things began to make.

With the book now completed, I realize just how much I owe to so many people, both in the writing of the book and the experiences it covers.

I owe the most to the people at the North Carolina Baptist Hospital. If it wasn't for you, I may not have been inspired to write at all. And I'm pretty sure if it wasn't for you, Rick would be lying under the grass today rather than walking on it. Our entire family thanks all of you from the bottom of our hearts. You are true heroes. Thank you, Dr. Michael Chang and the entire trauma team. And all of you nurses, too. Some of you didn't like me at times, and I've thought about apologizing for being a little pushy, but then again, I know you understand. And to the therapists and nurses in the Sticht Rehab Center, thank you. And thank you, Dr. Amy Olson. You helped me immensely, through some strange silent communication. If you didn't know it before, you do now. You never really said that much, but you didn't have to. For that I thank you.

My thanks to Bob Carlson and Porsche Cars North America. It is truly amazing just how compassionate you were when the chips were down. For a global company like Porsche to step up to bat for us was nothing short of amazing. Oh, and one more thing. Thanks for building the best sports cars in the world. It is a pleasure just to sit in one on the street. And pure joy kicking ass in one on the racetrack. My thanks to everyone who helped with the benefit for Rick: Bob Brooks, Jim Kenzie, and Bob Carlson and Susan Marsili of Porsche Cars North America. And to all those who donated items for the silent auction and all those – 350 strong – who attended.

Thank you, Mom, for instilling in me the bullheaded stubborn son-of-a-bitch attitude that helps me every day. Thank you for teaching me that falling down is not failing, but failing to get back up is. I'm sure there are days you wish I wasn't so stubborn. But remember, you made me this way. Some may not have appreciated it during the crisis Rick faced, but there were times when it was the only thing that got us through.

Thank you, Dad, for taking me to Mosport when I was five years old to watch my first race, and for all the times after that. During those times I came to know I would grow up to be a race-car driver. Thank you for all your support in helping me get there.

Thank you, Ken, older brother by three years and fighting coach.

Losing most of our fights sparked the desire in me to never give up ... and to always get even.

Thank you, Cathy and Hailey, wife and daughter. I love you both so much. Of all the people who have made my life amazing, you two have made it the most.

And thank you, Rick, older brother by seven years, for teaching me the meaning of the word *tenacity*. Your dogged desire and unwillingness to give up when it came to racing taught me a lesson that helps me every day. It has helped me on the racetrack, but more importantly it helped me help you. I guess that was my payback.

1

BROKEN

The best it can be pieced together – from details given by people who were involved, by others who came upon the scene moments later, and by the state police and emergency teams who were called in to clean up the whole mess – it happened like this.

It was a sunny day, around noon, on Thursday, January 29, 1998. Traveling southbound on Interstate 77 near Statesville, North Carolina, were the usual suspects: local townspeople and farmers, truckers hell-bent on making their schedules, and snowbirds being drawn as if by a magnet to Florida two states below.

My brother, Rick, was driving his pickup truck, with Rob, one of his race crew, riding shotgun. I'm sure Rick was relishing the prospect of racing his new Ford Mustang, which was inside the forty-eight-foot Pace American trailer he was pulling, at Daytona. This would be the first time in perhaps twenty years that he would be racing a non-Porsche race car.

Now, an F-350 pickup with a diesel engine has plenty enough torque to get a trailer that size moving. But as Rick and Rob were about to find out, it does not have nearly enough braking power to stop it quickly.

They were not too far from the end of their 1,000-mile trip from Oakville, Ontario, to Daytona Beach, Florida. Rick was scheduled to be on the track that very day to practice with his Commercial Motorsport race team for the 1998 Rolex 24 Hours at Daytona race. He was running late, as usual.

The two had just stopped at a truck stop for a bite to eat and a shower to help them freshen up.

Now, with Rob asleep in the passenger seat and Rick relaxed in the driver's seat, the Ford Dually easily climbed the north side of a long hill on the interstate. As the truck crested the hill, Rick expected his view of blue sky to be replaced with blacktop stretching all the way to the next hill. Instead, it was filled with the back end of two parked semi trucks sitting side by side, waiting for traffic to clear.

I have a pretty good idea of what happened next. Unlike most drivers, who would have panicked, Rick would have taken a deep breath and thought, "Okay, this is not very good." Rick had made his living as a professional race-car driver for the past twenty-five years or so. He had been in predicaments like this many times before. The difference this time was that he wasn't wearing his helmet and fire-proof racing suit. And he wasn't driving a Porsche.

My guess, he calmly looked to the right and then to the left for an escape route. He knew there was no way in hell he had time to stop the sixty-foot beast he was in control of. He would have focused and weighed his options. After trying them all and seeing that none of them would work, he would have calmly lain down across the front seat knowing damn well his trailer would soon be coming through the Dually's cab.

Rick was right. The impact was so powerful that the roof of the pickup was shorn clean off. A rear axle of one of the semis flew a hundred feet. The inertia from Rick's truck and trailer pushed that semi far enough ahead to involve a total of seven cars in the accident.

Why does it happen so often that one passenger in a serious accident walks away unhurt while the other, who was sitting right beside him, does not? Rob, Rick's passenger, was the lucky former. Rick was the unlucky latter.

Rob had come to with a sudden jolt forward as Rick hit the brakes of the Dually. I'm sure Rick knew that they were useless, but hell, he might as well try. It became apparent to Rob that they were not stopping, so he did what any sane, clear-thinking adult should do in such a situation. He undid his seatbelt. When asked later why he did that, he said, "Because I knew that when we hit, our trailer was going to take the cab off the truck so I'd better head for the floor." Good thinking. It probably saved his life.

When the noise subsided, Rob opened his eyes, like a child hiding under his bed thinking it was safe to come out – the boogie man had just left.

Blue sky, quiet ... and smoke. Looking up from the floor to where the roof used to be, all Rob saw was ... heaven? Not sure. Parts attached? Arm. Leg. Head. Umm, feel okay, but surely I can't be okay. Something must be broken.

A slow warm trickle trails down his forehead and along his nose, dripping off the tip. Blood. Okay, I'm not okay.

Voices: "Oh my God, is anyone in there? Can you hear me?"

"Get me the hell outta here," Rob says.

"Is there anyone else in there with you?"

"Yes, just get me the outta here. There's smoke – is this thing on fire?"

"Okay, hang on. We'll be right there. How many others are in there?"

"One. Rick."

"How is he?"

"Not very good."

The driver of one of the semis got his fire extinguisher and put out the fire that had started under Rick's hood. Looking inside the wreckage, he was sure no one could have survived. He was convinced that he was looking at a ghost, or two.

The accident put an end to any other travelers' plans for that day, at least if they were southbound on I-77 behind the mess. Their side of the highway was closed for hours.

The drivers of the wreckers stood around waiting like vultures for their chance to get at the wreckage. But the police waved them off as they interviewed those involved in the accident and those who had witnessed it.

Meanwhile, the emergency crews were working feverishly to tend to the people in need of medical care: one lady with a broken leg, Rob with a superficial cut on his head and a broken collar bone, although they didn't know that at the time, and Rick, who was bent, broken, and crushed in his twisted pile of metal.

Rick had taken the brunt of the impact and was stuck behind the wheel of his truck, unrecognizable. He faded in and out of consciousness as the emergency crew worked for forty-five minutes to free him. Then the emergency medical team took over. They put him in a helicopter and rushed him north to North Carolina Baptist Hospital in Winston-Salem just a few minutes away.

Horrible accidents have come to be expected by the people who live in the towns clustered along the highways that cut through the state, but this one was pretty big news and made the local broadcasts and newspapers.

It also made international sporting news. Porsche people all over the world heard about the crash. Rick's peers were shocked, despite the fact that his and their lives were in mortal danger every time they strapped on a helmet and nosed onto the track for their first lap, whether in practice or qualifying or competition.

Daytona International Speedway became ghostly quiet as the news spread. For perhaps the first time in their lives, many of the drivers didn't care whether they raced or not. The magic was gone. The usual excitement of the racetrack had turned to tears.

According to the hospital, there was a two percent chance that Rick would be coming out of that ER alive. A ninety-eight percent chance of not making it are odds that racers can understand. That's about the same odds they won't win Daytona, though that doesn't keep them from coming back year after year.

There was a moment of silence before the start of the race. A moment of silence in which a question vied in the racers' minds with their last-second hopes and excitement. And that question was how Rick Bye, a skilled race-car driver who had never been seriously hurt during his twenty-five-year career, could be fighting for his life in a hospital, the victim of a highway accident, instead of being there with them, preparing himself for that sweetest feeling of all: the adrenaline rush that follows the words, "Gentlemen, start your engines."

2
CATCHING
THE FEVER

Summer 1965 was the first time I went to a motor car race. I had just turned five and the venue was Mosport International Raceway, in Bowmanville, Ontario. Dad had packed our Ford Econoline van with all of our camping gear and thrown us three kids – Rick, twelve, Ken, eight, and me, five – in the back. With Mom beside him in the front, off we went. I have no idea how long it took to drive the hundred miles from St. Catharines to the track in that old van, but I am sure it was a while.

I really don't remember a lot about my first racetrack experience, but I do remember one thing: standing with Rick at the top of corner 2 looking through the fence and seeing the cars coming out of corner 1 and down the short straight at us.

Cars had always been a part of my life, but not ones like these at the racetrack. Dad was in the automotive business and I often went to the shop on weekends to help out – or more accurately to get in the way. I would grab a broom and push it around until I got bored, which for this five year old was probably after two minutes. I would grab Dad's tools and work on whatever car or truck was parked inside the shop. Inevitably I would get grease on my pants or shirt and Mom would yell at Dad for not watching me.

After helping set up the camp around the van I had gone to the fence and tried to look through it. All I could see were people, tall people. They were lined up along the fence as far as I could see. The ones around us must have felt us standing at the back of their legs because they moved aside to let us through. Once we got to the front of the crowd, we couldn't see Dad, though I'm sure he could see us.

At first I didn't hear anything, but everyone in the crowd leaned forward as if they had. I looked up, tilted my head backwards – everyone was looking to the left – or was it right? Oh well – doesn't matter. Then the ground started to shake. What was that noise? It couldn't be cars. Cars don't make sounds like that. A flash of color came into view as about thirty Can-Am cars came sailing out of turn 1 to begin their first practice lap.

As the cars got closer, the sound became deafening and my body started to shake along with the ground. I stepped back a little out of fear but mostly out of awe. These cars were unlike any cars I had ever seen. And at five years old I knew every car on the road. *WWWAN* ... *WWWWAN* ... *WWWAN, WWAN, WWAN, WWANWWANWWAN* – these big, giant beasts flew past where I was standing. The ground shook even more as well as the trees and the cars parked in the infield of corner 2.

As the noise of the cars diminished, the cheers of the crowd came to life. Everyone was yelling and screaming and holding up their beer bottles. (It would take some years for me to learn that race fans and beer go hand-in-hand.)

A shiver went down my spine and I knew right then and there what I was going to be when I grew up. I was going to be a race-car driver. I remember looking up at Rick standing beside me. He had the very same look on his face. He would start down that road six years before me, in 1972, when he was eighteen and I was just eleven.

Ken was there, too, but he didn't seem to share the same interest in racing. I think he just had better sense than we did, somehow escaping the racing fever.

In the spring of 1977, just after my seventeenth birthday, I attended a three-day racing school at Shannonville Motorsport Park, Shannonville, Ontario. This is where I would eventually get my professional racing license. Rick had supplied me with a brand new Formula Vee for the weekend. I was on cloud nine. I had to work at his shop to help pay off my debt to him, which was okay with me because at my tender age I didn't have any money.

Over the next several years Rick and I slowly climbed the motorsport ladder. Rick was always several rungs ahead of me, partly because he had a head start and partly because he was more focused than I was. You see, Rick had never discovered beer, and I had. I had discovered motorcycles and spent off-weekends riding my bike and drinking beer with my buddies. Rick spent his off-weekends testing and working on his race car.

Rick eventually graduated to Super Vee and then on to Porsche. As soon as he got hooked up with Porsche, in 1986, things started to happen in his career. While he focused on sports car racing with Porsche, I remained focused on open-wheel cars like Formula Fords and Formula 2000s. I liked the challenge of driving these cars even though it's harder to build a career racing them compared with sports cars.

— — —

It was in the early 1980s, after Rick and I had been racing for a few years, that I learned my first real lesson in just how cruel racing can be. To that point I had never even given a second thought to the fact that racing was dangerous. A friend and fellow Formula Vee competitor had moved on up the racing ladder. His name was Peter Moenick. We raced against each other during the racing season and then went skiing together in the winter. Peter was much older than I was but we always had a good time hanging out. Peter had two sons. Derrick was about thirteen and Mitchell was five or six.

In 1981 Peter was racing a Porsche 911 in the Molson 100 Camel GT race at Mosport. He had recently taken the big step of moving from Formula Vee to Endurance racing in a Porsche, but he had more than enough talent to handle it.

No one really knows what happened that fateful day, but partway into the race, Peter's Porsche slammed into the outside retaining wall at corner 4 – a place where you really don't want anything to go wrong because you are flying. This corner can be taken flat out in some cars and at a hundred miles per hour in just about anything. Corner 4 at Mosport is exhilarating in any type of car. Done well there is no better feeling than flying over the top of the hill, flat out. Done wrong – well, you just never know.

Peter died that day. As with just about every racing accident it was announced that he died of his injuries on the way to the hospital. It is rare that a race-car driver is ever announced dead at the scene. Promoters or owners of a racetrack don't want to have a death at the track. I guess that makes sense. Peter's youngest son, Mitchell, grabbed onto Rick's pant leg and asked, "Where are they taking my dad?" as Peter was rushed off to the hospital by ambulance. "He's gonna be all right, though, right Rick?" Rick looked down at Mitch, patted him on the back, and quietly said, "I hope so."

Peter was the first friend that this sport – the sport we loved so much – took from Rick and me. And he would not be the last. Rick and I never talked about Peter after that. We never talked about missing him or even what we thought caused the accident. I guess it didn't really matter to us exactly what went wrong. Or perhaps, more accurately, we just didn't want to know.

I went on to purchase Peter's Formula Vee from his widow, Kay, that year. She gave me a deal and said Peter would have wanted me to have it. I always felt Peter was there, beside me, holding his right foot on top of mine, not letting me lift it when I wanted to. Sometimes Derrick came by our trailer in the paddock and asked if he could sit in his dad's car.

"Sure," I would reply, "and you stay in there as long as you like."

We didn't see much of Mitchell after that day. I think he was just too young to deal with his dad's death. Kay never came back to the track. At least not that I know of.

3
"DON'T COME HERE"

On that Thursday afternoon in January I was in my office at Franczak Enterprises in Markham, Ontario, on the northeastern edge of Toronto, with my partner and friend Hank Franczak.

The phone rang. Hank leaned over, answered it, and handed it to me across the desk.

As I took the phone I looked out the window to check on how hard it was snowing.

"Chris." I couldn't quite place the voice. "Chris, it's Ken," the caller said.

It was strange for Ken, my brother, to be calling me at work. He was calling from Commercial Auto Electric in St. Catharines where he worked with Dad. Commercial was the largest Ford Motorcraft distributor in Canada. Motorcraft was Ford's aftermarket parts line. Commercial had about eight service bays where general vehicle repairs were done. I had left just the year before to pursue working with Franczak Enterprises Ltd. full time. Rick had left many years earlier. He and Dad used to fight like hell at work. Family businesses can be tough. Rick and Dad got along famously after they stopped working together.

"There's been an accident," Ken said quietly. "It's Rick."

"What do you mean?"

"I'm not sure. We just got a call from Aunt Midge and she said Rick was in an accident on his way to Daytona."

"Where? How bad?" I asked.

"I don't know, but I have a phone number."

"Give it to me. I'll call you back. Have you talked to Mom and Dad?"

"Yeah, I'm at work with Dad. He knows. Make sure you call me back," he said.

I dialed the number Ken gave me and a man answered.

"Who's this?" I asked.

"Bill, it's Bill. Who's this?"

"Bill who?"

"Bill Hoeffle."

I had no clue who the hell Bill was. That was not unusual. Rick regularly had dozens of new people hanging around his shop helping him prepare his team's cars. We found out later that Bill had been following Rick in his Mustang. He and his passenger, another member of Rick's crew, had been stuck in traffic and were horrified to see that a big black Ford F-350 with a forty-eight-foot trailer attached – just like the one they had been following since leaving Oakville, Ontario, the day before – was in the accident that caused the traffic jam.

"Bill, this is Chris, Rick's brother. Are you with Rick?"

"Well, no, not exactly."

"Bill, where the hell are you?"

"On the side of the road."

It was obvious that Bill was in shock. He had no idea who I was or why I was calling. His voice sounded hollow. I could tell he was on a cell phone and was wandering around outside. I could hear cars going by as he was talking to people.

"Bill, where are you?" I asked again.

"I'm not sure. I think somewhere in North Carolina."

"Bill, where is Rick? Is he there with you?"

"No, they took him away," he said in a whisper.

"Who took him? Where?"

"The guys in the helicopter, this guy and a girl, they took him in the helicopter."

I didn't know till that moment what people meant when they

said that their heart sank. I sat back in my chair and tried to catch the breath that had just left my mouth and would not return.

One of Rick's best friends was Ruedi Hafen from Niagara Helicopters. Rick and I had spent a lot of time flying to and from various places and racetracks with Ruedi. I knew the helicopter ride Bill was referring to was unlike any Rick had taken before. In the racing world it was never good news when the two words "accident" and "helicopter" were used in the same sentence.

"Bill, is there anyone there I can talk to?"

"Um, yeah, just a minute," Bill replied.

I looked across my desk at Hank for the first time since getting on the line. He looked me with a concern I had never seen from him before. Then he left the room to give me some privacy.

Bill came back on. "Chris, everyone's kinda busy. It's a bit of a mess around here."

"Bill, ask someone what town you're in."

A few moments later: "Statesville, we're in Statesville, North Carolina."

"Thanks, Bill. Keep your phone on. I'll call you back."

I wasn't sure what to do next. A phone book sitting on a table across the room came into focus. I opened it to the area code section and looked for Statesville, North Carolina.

It wasn't there, no area code for Statesville. Lovely. What about Charlotte? It couldn't be far from Charlotte. I wonder how big North Carolina is? It couldn't be that big, could it? Charlotte is 704. Statesville must be the same. I dialed long distance information.

"What city and state, please?"

"Statesville, North Carolina."

"Can I help you?"

"Yeah, the Statesville sheriff's office."

"Sir, please hold for the number."

I dialed the number given.

"Statesville Sheriff's Office, how may I direct your call?" asked a female voice in a clear southern accent.

"I'm not sure," I began. "I believe that my brother has been involved in an accident in or around Statesville."

"Sir, can I have your name?"

"Chris Bye."

"Mr. Bye, what's your brother's name?"

"Rick, Richard Bye."

"Okay, Mr. Bye, please hold the line."

A deputy speaking in a male version of that southern accent came on the line. "Mr. Bye, there has been a multi-vehicle accident in the southbound lanes of I-77 near the intersection of I-40. Do you know what type of vehicle your brother was driving?"

"Yeah, a black Ford Dually pickup."

"Was he pulling a big white trailer?"

"Yeah."

"Oh ... Mr. Bye, could you hold the line for a moment?"

I pulled the phone away from my ear and looked at it. I have no idea what I thought I might see. I put it back to my ear, wondering what was being said in the room at the other end of the line.

"Mr. Bye, there has been an accident that involved about seven cars. It appears at this time that your brother's truck was involved. I can't tell you anything on his status, but I can tell you that he has been transferred to the North Carolina Baptist Hospital in Winston-Salem by AirCare."

"Were you there? Do you know how he is?"

"I'm sorry, Mr. Bye. I don't know anything more than what I have told you."

I wasted no time dialing the number he gave me for the hospital.

For possibly the first time in my life I didn't mind being put on hold. I would have been happy to just sit there and listen to the elevator music for the rest of my life.

I was finally put through to the ER where a nurse identified herself as Amy, the AirCare nurse who had helped take Rick to the hospital.

"How is he?" I asked. "What happened? Is he all right?"

"Rick is with the trauma team right now and all I can tell you is that he couldn't be in better hands."

"What are his injuries?"

"I'm sorry. I really can't tell you much about his injuries. The trauma team will have some answers for you as soon as they stabilize him and determine their extent."

"Can you at least tell me what happened?"

"Well, I can tell you that he was involved in a multi-vehicle accident. EMT was onsite in about four minutes and we got there shortly after that. EMT worked for about forty-five minutes to free him from the wreckage and I was there the entire time holding his hand."

"Was he conscious?"

"Well, sort of. He was awake, but not really alert. In fact the only thing he would say was yes. If I asked him if he was okay or if I asked him where he was, the answer was the same: yes. We got him free and placed him in the helicopter. He became very agitated in the helicopter and somewhat combative. That's very common for someone who has suffered these types of injuries."

"What type of injuries?" I asked, hoping to catch her off guard.

"As I said earlier, I really can't tell you much at this point. Let me see if I can find someone who can tell you more. Just hang on a minute."

A man came on identifying himself as a doctor on the trauma team that was taking care of Rick.

"Mr. Bye, Rick is very sick and we are doing everything in our power to make him as comfortable as possible. He has a closed-head injury, among other things."

"A closed-head injury?"

"That's a head injury where there is no visible damage. You know, like a really bad bump on the head."

"Is there any swelling?"

"We're not sure. The first seventy-two hours are crucial, Chris. We will monitor him closely for that time for sure."

"What else?" I asked impatiently.

"He has a significant fracture of his left hip and he also has an open fracture of his right ankle."

"Is that it?"

"He has a number of scrapes and contusions. As I said, we are still working on him. That's about all I can tell you at this time."

"I'll check on flights and we'll be there just as soon as we can."

"Chris."

"Yeah?"

"Don't come here."

"Pardon me?"

"Look, Chris, don't come down here, please. Just sit tight. We'll call you just as soon as we have a better handle on Rick's condition."

I didn't have an answer for that. I knew all too well what he was getting at – that things were going very badly and were probably going to get a lot worse before they got better. If they did get better.

– – –

"Commercial," my dad said, the way he always answers the phone at his business. Dad had started the company in the 1960s when Rick, Ken, and I were just kids. He was a truck mechanic for a transport company when one day he removed the door from my bedroom to use as a work bench in our basement. That was the beginning of his company. Since that time it grew to become a major part of the automotive industry in St. Catharines.

St. Catharines is a town of about one hundred twenty-five thousand people on Lake Ontario just northwest of Niagara Falls. Everyone in the automotive business in the area knew us. Commercial had given Rick and me the opportunity to pursue our racing careers. The company had not spent a lot of money on us, but they gave us a shop and equipment to use in developing and maintaining our own race cars.

"I'm not really sure what's going on, but I think we need to get down there," I said.

"Do you want to fly?"

"No, I already called the airlines and we can't get out until 8 tomorrow morning. I looked at the atlas and it's about 600 miles. If we leave now we can be there by morning."

Next I got my wife, Cathy, on the line. She manages a store for Shoppers Drug Mart in St. Catharines.

"Hey, how are you?" she said in her normal bubbly voice.

"There's been an accident. It's Rick. He's been airlifted to a hospital in Winston-Salem, North Carolina. I am heading out right now. There are no flights so we'll drive. We'll pick up Mom and Dad and hit the road as soon as I get home. Can you take care of Hailey and Riley?"

"How is he?"

"I don't know, but I don't think it's good. He has a head injury and it took the EMT forty-five minutes to cut him out of the truck. They told us not to come there."

"Was he alone?"

"No, there was one other guy in the truck. It seems that he's okay."

"How are you?" she asked.

"I'm okay. I just want to get down there."

"Hey."

"Yeah?"

"Drive carefully," she said quietly.

"I will. See you in a bit."

The drive from my office in Markham to St. Catharines is about 110 miles. Normally it's not such a bad drive, but that day, the first real snowstorm of the New Year, it really sucked. There hadn't been even a hint of bad weather that morning, which is why I had taken my 5.0 liter Mustang out of storage for the day's drive. The only thing worse than driving a Mustang in the snow is driving a Mustang in the snow through Toronto traffic. It took me two and a half hours to make the one-and-a-half-hour trip.

As I was heading home, Cathy picked up our six-year-old daughter, Hailey, at school and took her to her parents' house a few minutes from ours. Then she dropped our dog Riley off at the kennel just one mile from our home. She made no arrangements with her mom or the kennel as to when she would pick up her charges. Would we be home in days, weeks, or months? We didn't know.

4
THE DRIVE
TO ETERNITY

The drive to North Carolina was long and quiet. It snowed the whole way. If we had been going skiing it would have been a perfect drive. Instead, it was like we were traveling into the twilight zone. The snow was hypnotic, almost comforting. The concentration required to drive in these conditions helped me keep my mind off things. But I couldn't help replaying those awful words: "Don't come here. We'll call you."

My head kept shaking involuntarily, as if it was trying to force those words out of my brain.

We were driving Cathy's 1997 Honda Civic. Cathy was by my side, and Mom and Dad were in the back seat. Ken needed to stay behind and help run things at Commercial. That way Dad could come down to Winston-Salem and stay as long as he needed to.

I had been driving for about eight hours and it was about 2 a.m. We had reached highway 19 heading south toward Beckley, West Virginia, after crossing the border at Queenston Lewiston and cutting through a swatch of western New York and Pennsylvania.

The conditions were getting worse. The night got darker as the mountains got higher. There was road construction all the way along highway 19. In fact, in my memory, that was the normal condition of this particular highway.

I couldn't keep my chin off my chest. The conditions were exhausting. I needed a break. After we stopped for gas, Cathy took the wheel.

It makes no sense, but the state of West Virginia uses very large barrels with fluorescent stripes on them as lane barriers for highways undergoing construction. At night these barrels are very distracting. They all run together and pretty soon you can't tell where one lane ends and another begins. As I drifted off to sleep, I thought, "This highway is an accident just waiting to happen."

It couldn't have been more than ten minutes later that I heard Cathy gasp. I bolted upright. We were off the road, heading for total blackness. To the left was the highway, to the right an exit ramp, straight ahead, who knows.

"Right, go right," I said as calmly as I could. Cathy did exactly what I hoped she would. She got hold of herself and turned to the right slowly and calmly. The car found the exit ramp and we exited the highway safely, slowing to a stop.

"Those damn barrels," she said, disappointed in herself.

"Jump out, I'll drive," I said. I was not the least bit upset with her, but I was too tired to tell her so.

A few minutes later the silence was broken by the exceptionally loud ringing of my father's cell phone. My mother nearly jumped out of her skin. Why is it that cell phones have such a loud ring, I wondered. My father fumbled with the phone, finally managing to answer it.

"Yeah, yeah, okay," was all he said before hitting the end button.

My mother was still trying to catch her breath and finally asked who it was. I felt numb, hoping he wouldn't answer. I didn't hear what he said, and that was fine by me. I figured if he thought I needed to know, he would tell me.

Darkness slowly turned to light. I had been behind the wheel for almost twelve hours and I felt like a zombie. I call it numb and dumb. In one way you feel like you could drive another thousand miles, but in another you feel you could sleep standing up in a hammock.

I smiled, recalling the same thing that always comes back to me when I have to drive tired.

— — —

It was the spring of 1978 and Rick and I had been racing at Shannonville Motorsport Park in Eastern Ontario. Rick was twenty-four by this time, and I was eighteen. Shannonville is about four and a half hours from our parents' home, where Rick and I were both living at the time. We sure couldn't afford to live on our own. At least not while we were spending the money racing that we were.

We always planned to leave the track right after the races but that never happened. This particular weekend we were trying to get the bugs out of a new race car that Rick had just purchased, a Formula Super Vee, powered by a 1600 cc Volkswagen engine. It was a big step up from the Formula Vees we had been racing.

We left the track way too late, as usual, probably around 9 p.m. Rick was in the lead, driving his truck and towing his race car. I followed in my pickup, towing my race car. I remember driving through Toronto on highway 401 praying that I would stay awake. All I could think of was how sweet it was going to be to climb into my bed. I continued along the 401 and onto the QEW toward Hamilton and St. Catharines.

Next thing I knew, a car behind me was laying on the horn. I had fallen asleep at the wheel at a stoplight on Niagara St. in St. Catharines, just off the highway. I looked into the mirror and all I could see were headlights. I looked ahead and saw that the light was green. I gathered my thoughts, and my dignity, and proceeded through the intersection slowly, trying to look cool. You know, like when you are sound asleep and someone calls you. The first thing they always ask is, "Did I wake you?" And you reply, "No, not at all, I'm fine."

My eyes were open now, all right. It was a good thing that the road went slightly uphill at the intersection or I might have rolled right through it.

I looked at my watch as I pulled in front of our house. It was 3 a.m. I had no idea how long I had been sitting at the light, asleep. Rick's truck was parked in front of the house. Judging by the volume of Rick's snores as I walked past his room, he had been asleep for some time.

The next morning I was sitting drinking coffee when Rick came into the kitchen.

"What happened to you last night?" he asked as he poured his coffee.

"Nothing. Why?" I said as I headed for the door, hiding a smile.

5

GLEAMING
HALLWAYS

"Welcome to Winston-Salem," the sign proclaimed. It was early Friday morning. We stopped at an Exxon station just off the highway for directions and then headed to North Carolina Baptist Hospital on the northern edge of town.

As we walked into the lobby of the hospital it was clear this place was not lacking for money, or if it was, the administrators were doing an expert job of hiding the fact. The hospital was like none I had ever seen in Canada. The lobby was more like a luxury hotel's. The ceiling was very high. There was a gift shop straight ahead and a desk to the right. Gleaming hallways spun off to the left and the right.

"Hi, can I help you?" a cheerful lady at the receptionist's desk asked.

"Yes, we're here to see Rick Bye," I said.

"Okay. Just a moment please."

"Nice place," my father said, looking up at the ceiling.

"Yeah, I'll say," I said. I turned to Cathy. "How ya doin'?" I asked.

"I'm okay. How are you?"

"I'm fine," I said, lying through my teeth. She knew it. In reality I was just a body with a brain that wouldn't stop replaying those words: "Don't come here. We'll call you."

I looked at my mother for probably the first time since we left home. I knew immediately that she was not up to seeing Rick.

Mom and I had hardly spoken for almost a year. I couldn't remember why. She and I were like that – we would go through times where we didn't talk. We seemed to get caught up in our own worlds and before we knew it, we were oceans apart. I don't think it was really a big deal to either one of us. It just happened. Perhaps it had something to do with the way she had brought me up. She had taught me to do whatever I chose in life and to never let anyone stand in my way. And that was pretty much how I had lived, just doing whatever I had to do to do whatever I wanted. If anyone didn't like it, oh well, they'll get over it. And if they didn't, oh well.

It was Mom who had told me from a very young age, "Do whatever you decide in life and if someone doesn't like it, tell them to kiss your ass. Even if it's me or your father." And that has pretty much been my motto. Not that I go out of my way to piss people off. It's just that I do what I want. And as long as it doesn't interfere or harm anyone else, then it's okay with me.

I hadn't spoken to Rick that much either, mainly because we were now on different paths.

At the end of the 1995 racing season I had been invited to test with an Indy Lights Team. I went to Big Springs, Texas, just a short drive from Midland, with several other Canadian drivers, Andrew Bordin, Lee Bentham, and a few others. We spent three days there driving the Indy Lights car owned by Brian Stewart Racing. I spent the next several months trying to find money to put an Indy Lights program together. But at that time I knew that the end of my racing career was near. I was thirty-five years old. My teammate in 1995, Rob MacDonald, was seventeen.

Earlier that year Rob and I were at Mosport and had just come off the track after a qualifying session and were talking with the team about making adjustments to the cars. I looked over to Rob and said, "You know what I just realized? The year you were born was the year I started racing."

"No way," Rob said as he looked over at his mom and dad.

"Yep," I said, "I started racing in 1977."

Rob just sat there and looked at me with a blank look on his face. "You're kidding, right?"

"Nope," I said with a grin as I grabbed a Diet Coke out of the cooler.

Since trying, unsuccessfully, to raise the money to go into Indy Lights racing, I had started to think about life without racing. It wasn't that I thought I would ever stop racing for good. I just realized that I was now officially too old.

One night I said to Cathy, "You know, if I am half as good at making money as I am at spending it, we'll probably be okay."

And that was when I decided to focus on work – with Franczak – and making a living. It was difficult to turn my back on the sport I loved so much. A sport that had been so much of my life. A sport that had introduced me to some of the most amazing people in the world. A sport that had been the thread between Rick and me.

In the two years that followed I focused on working. Rick was still focused on doing his thing, racing and managing the Porsche press car fleet. Rick took care of Porsche's press cars for Eastern Canada. Whenever journalists in Ontario or Quebec wanted to drive a Porsche for a story, they would get that car from Rick. He made sure the car was detailed and mechanically perfect before delivering it to them. Rick felt he had the best job in the world. And so did a lot of other people.

The distance between us grew even more when he ended his nine-year relationship with Wendy, the daughter of my business partner, Hank. She had basically been a part of our family over the past decade or so. The fact that they had split up had no bearing whatsoever on how I and the rest of our family felt about her. She was still family. Hank and I had never spoken about Rick and Wendy's relationship. We had always respected the fact that this subject was too close to home to discuss.

Initially, Hank was somewhat uncomfortable with their relationship. He had hoped his daughter would meet someone who could give her a comfortable life and financial security. Rick was definitely not that person. He was way too selfish and focused on of his racing career to support anyone.

Despite our distance, it was Rick who got me to give in and eventually call Mom.

"Mr. Bye. ICU 5B. Rick is in ICU 5B," the receptionist said. "You go down the hall and take the elevators up to the fifth floor. When you exit the elevators on the fifth floor, turn right and go past the waiting room. Turn left at the end of the hall and go down to 5B, you'll see it on the door. There will be a phone on the wall beside the door. Pick it up and the nurse inside will answer it. Just tell them your name and they will let you in."

Many other people in the hallways seemed as confused as we were. We somehow found our way to the sign for room 5B and I picked up the phone outside the wide double doors.

"5B," a voice said.

"Hi, this is the Bye family. We're here to see Rick."

"Okay. Just wait there and I'll be right out to speak to you."

We stood there in our own little worlds. We didn't know, and didn't really want to know, what was waiting for us.

Finally the doors swung open and a nurse came out. As if at some kind of party, I said to her politely, "Hi, I'm Chris Bye, Rick's brother. This is my wife, Cathy, and my parents, Richard and Edna."

The nurse started right into the procedure for seeing Rick. "Okay, I just want to let you know what to expect when you go in there. The first thing you will notice as you approach Rick is all of the machines that he's hooked up to. He has an ICP bolt in and that may be a little disturbing."

"An ICP bolt?" I asked.

"It's a plastic bolt that is inserted into his head to monitor his ICP numbers."

"ICP numbers?"

"Measurements of Internal Cranial Pressure," she said. "His left leg is broken, so there's an apparatus over his bed holding his leg. He has a feeding tube in and he's also on a respirator. Please just ask any questions that come to you."

The room was long and narrow. There were ten or twelve beds lined up along the outside walls. We walked along quietly until the nurse stopped at a bed just across from the nurses' desk. The only reason we stopped was because the nurse had stopped. But slowly it dawned on us that the person in the bed beside us must be Rick.

The first thing I noticed was the large plastic bolt screwed into the right side of his head, which had been shaved. The bolt was attached to a wire and the wire went behind the bed to a panel of monitors. Rick's face was swollen beyond recognition and covered with scrapes and bruises. His whole body was covered by a clean white sheet.

Several tubes were coming out from under the sheet. Or were they going in? Rick's left leg was in traction, held high off the bed. My eyes continued down to the end of the bed and then back up. About halfway back up my eyes stopped. I was sure the angle of his right foot was nowhere near right. I didn't have the nerve to look back down.

I don't know how long I was standing there before I realized that what I was hearing came from what I was seeing.

Click, besheeeh.

Click, besheeeh.

Click, besheeeh. Rick's chest rose.

Click, besheeeh. Rick's chest dropped.

I turned to where the sound was coming from and saw a small machine behind the left side of his bed. The face of the machine was covered in dials and gauges. The tube coming out it went straight into Rick's mouth. It hit me: Rick was on life support. This machine was breathing for him. I looked back at the machine and then my eyes followed the electrical cord to the wall. For the first time I realized the true meaning of pulling the plug. It would be just that simple. Just pull that plug and it's all over.

I looked around the room and realized that more people than not were hooked up to these machines. In the bed right next to Rick was a handsome Spanish kid who looked to be about twenty-five. He had a long shiny black ponytail that was neatly placed over his left shoulder. His body was totally covered, except for his hands, which were lying perfectly flat at his side, his fingers positioned an equal distance apart.

Something about him was very different from Rick. He seemed not to have any trauma, and nothing was in traction. Both of his feet were pointing in the right direction, toward the ceiling. He looked so peaceful, so normal, like someone in a deep sleep. Except normal people who are sleeping don't have perfect hair. They don't have their hands placed perfectly at their sides. And they don't have a machine beside them going *click, besheeeh, click besheeeh.*

I looked at what I would learn was the "pod." It sat at the head of Rick's bed and went from floor to ceiling. It had as many tubes and connections as it had dials and gauges.

Dad was staring at Rick with no emotion. He was blank. Mom was a different story. Her eyes were wide open and she was covering her mouth with her right hand. Her eyes made contact with mine but she didn't see me. I don't think she could see anything but Rick, and who could blame her? That was her baby lying there, bent, broken, crushed, and twisted.

Click, besheeeh, click besheeeh brought my eyes back to Rick's chest. Up, pause. Down, pause. Up, pause. Down, pause.

I got a strange feeling that someone else was in the ICU looking at Rick and us, and sure enough, there, standing just off to the end of Rick's bed, was Kathryn. I knew very little about her, just that she was a race-car driver who had been around Rick after his recent breakup with Wendy. I took an instant dislike to her. I think I was probably frustrated that Rick had left Wendy. I was also feeling territorial about anyone seeing Rick in this state. If we, his family, hadn't fully processed what had happened to him, why would we want strangers in on the process?

Kathryn moved closer to the bed and introduced herself to my parents. She said hello to Cathy before cautiously looking at me.

Cathy says I don't have to say a word to anyone I don't like – it's written all over my face. She says if someone I don't like walks into a room, the temperature plummets. I know what she means, and I have tried not to show whatever it is that I show, but I guess I still need some practice.

Kathryn began to explain that she had headed to the hospital right after hearing the details of the accident and had been there all night. She went on to say that the blistering on Rick's face was from the fluid they were giving him through his IV. She told us that the doctors said the blistering would get much worse before it got better.

Well that's just great. That's just what we all needed to hear right then, more bad news. Somehow I managed to keep my mouth shut.

I asked a nurse if we could speak to a doctor.

"The doctors have been notified that you're here," she told me. "They will be by as soon as they're able."

The entire nursing staff in the ICU seemed to be aware of everything around them. Like waitresses in a five-star restaurant, they gave us space but were never far away if we needed anything.

We hadn't been at Rick's bedside very long when Mom and Dad said they were going out to get some air. That meant that my mother was going out for a cigarette. I sure couldn't blame her at that point – hell, I felt like going out for a smoke myself and I hate cigarettes.

Cathy looked over at me. "You want to go for a walk?"

"No, I'm okay. You go," I replied.

"Are you sure?"

"I'm fine. You go."

Cathy knew I wanted some time to be alone. She also knew that no matter what was about to happen to us over the next several days, weeks, and months, I would never break down in front of anyone, not even her.

She smiled a loving smile as she tilted her head. "I won't be far," she said as she took my hand and squeezed it.

I didn't know what was going to happen when I tried to talk to Rick, but I ventured in.

"Hey man, it's Chris. You look pretty screwed up. I bet all that shit hurts. Remember what I said the first time I rode your Harley? It might be ugly, but it is slow. Well I hate to tell you, but you look pretty ugly right now, too."

I watched his face, hoping for a grin, or more appropriately a "screw you."

Click, besheeeh, click besheeeh was the only response I got.

I was close enough now to see that his mouth, which was held partly open by the tubes going in, was full of dried blood. There was so much blood that I couldn't see his teeth, if there were any. I walked down toward the end of his bed and somehow found the nerve to lift the sheets up at his feet. His legs were as black as coal.

Man, how are you going to get out of this one?

I don't know how long I stood there. Cathy came back into the ICU. "How ya doing?" she asked.

I just gave her a rueful smile and a shoulder shrug. She tilted her head and the corners of her mouth curled up as she gave me one of those "it's going to be okay" looks. I saw my parents coming back into the ICU.

They were not doing so well.

"Why don't you go take a break?" Mom said to me.

"Okay, but come and get me if the doctors come in."

"Don't worry, we will."

6

FAMILY TIES

My earliest memories of Rick are of him riding off on his dirt bike. Ever since I can remember he always had a toy of some sort or another. And he was forever working on building or fixing something: model cars, go karts, bikes, or slot car tracks. If any of the neighborhood kids ever broke anything, they would bring it to Rick to fix. Since Rick was so much older than I was, we didn't really hang out that much. When I was five he was twelve. And the last thing any twelve year old wants is to have to drag their five-year-old brother around with them. Ken was a different story. Since he was only three years older than I was, Mom would make him take me places. He hated this. He used to make me walk a hundred feet behind him and his friends. They would take off and run away and stand back and laugh as I tried to catch up.

Being forced to take care of me must be why Ken was always fighting with me. But even though Ken would kick my ass at the drop of a hat, one thing was sure: he was the first to take on any of the neighborhood kids who were picking on me. I would run straight to him and he would take care of them.

Once, when I was eleven or twelve, I challenged Ken to a boxing match on our front lawn. This was possibly one of the dumbest things I have ever done. As we prepared for the match, just about every kid around came over to our house to watch the excitement. I can't remember where we got the boxing gloves, but I do remember that they were the most pathetic, lame, limp ones I had ever seen. "This is probably not a good idea," I thought as I put the gloves on. The boxing gloves on TV looked big and soft and fluffy. How much could they possibly hurt? These weren't anything like that.

Ken stood at one corner of the lawn, gloves on, grinning from ear to ear at me standing at the other corner. "Ding! Ding!" one of the kids from across the street yelled. I figured if I put my head down and charged, swinging wildly, I might land one and he would go down. Well, okay, I didn't think he would go down, but I was determined to land at least one. Then, all of a sudden, before I could take a swing, *bam*, a shocking pain traveled through my head from one ear to the other. Just as I attempted to gather my thoughts and my balance, *bam*, my knees weakened as some son of a bitch moved the jack hammer that had just hit me and lined it up dead center on the top of my head. As my knees gave out I could hear all the kids gathering around laughing.

I staggered to get out of Ken's range. He was killing himself laughing.

"Come on, tough guy," he said. I did my best not to cry in front of our audience. I would never have lived it down if I had let Ken bring me to tears. Especially since the whole idea was mine in the first place. I gathered my composure and somehow talked my way out of any further right hooks. To this day I don't know if any of my bombs ever landed. Well, okay, maybe they weren't bombs.

— — —

When I think of the highlights of our childhood, I remember, fondly, the trips to Florida in our big Oldsmobile Delta 88. We had to spend every other night sleeping in the car because we couldn't afford a hotel room every night. Before the trip, our parents sat us all down and explained that this was the only way we could go. Since I was the youngest, I got the back window. Rick got the back seat and Ken got the floor ... with the hump. Mom and Dad slept in their respective front seats, waking up, I'm sure, as stiff as boards. There must have been days when they thought, "What the hell are we doing?"

How many parents would sleep in their cars every other night for two weeks so they could take their kids south? No fancy restaurants for us, either, just lunches consisting of dry bread and bologna. We would find some quiet, secluded piece of beach or river bank somewhere and break out the picnic blanket. We would share a large bottle of root beer and Mom would put together our sandwiches. We would skip rocks on the water and feed the birds and fish the leftover bread.

One time when Ken was throwing bread crumbs to the fish he noticed a big log floating toward the beach. Only this log had teeth – big teeth. This log was a living, breathing alligator and it came up on the beach where we were sitting. Ken grabbed a knife out of Dad's tackle box and said, "If that thing takes one more step toward us, I'm going to stab it right between the eyes." At that moment the gator opened his mouth as wide as it could, hissed, and took a few steps forward. Ken was the first one to run – he headed straight for the woods. The rest of us screamed and ran toward the car. The gator just lay there with his mouth wide open, hissing. It took us a couple of minutes to realize that it wasn't interested in eating us. We probably smelled too bad.

Finally, Ken came back out of the woods and Mr. Gator went back into the water. We spent the rest of the day laughing and daring each other to go swimming. Then we drove to a truck stop to get cleaned up and get ready to go to sleep in the truck stop parking lot.

The thing I remember most about growing up was Dad working too much. But back in those days just about everyone's father worked too much. Mom stayed home and took care of three maniac boys. I'm sure there were times when she wondered what the hell she had got herself into, having three boys. Mom and Dad had a lot of friends. They used to have a lot of parties, playing Johnny Cash records and dancing late into the night. They were always good about letting us stay up past our bedtime and hang around with the adults. From what I remember, they didn't have much choice. If they made us go to bed, we would just sneak out of our bedrooms and go downstairs.

Our driving experience got off to an early start, thanks to Ken, a good friend of our parents who visited regularly. As he sat and chatted at the kitchen table he would announce that he was going to the store. Whenever us kids heard him say that, we would come running.

"Can we come, too, Ken?" we would ask with the excitement of Christmas morning in our voices.

"Sure," he would reply and start laughing as he looked at Mom.

"Ken, don't you let him drive," she would say as I struggled to get my shoes on.

"Who me?" Ken replied, giving me a wink.

"Ken, I'm serious, don't let him drive," she'd say again as we headed out the door. Ken would get into the driver's seat as I got into the passenger seat. Mom would be looking out the front door shaking her finger at him. He'd wave and laugh as loud as hell. The moment we were around the corner, he'd pull over to the curb and I would jump across the seat and grab the steering wheel. I couldn't reach the pedals, so Ken operated them as I steered. I would drive all the way to the store and back.

As we approached our house, Ken would make me get back over into the passenger seat. As we pulled into our driveway, he'd say, "Now don't tell your mother I let you drive."

"I won't," I'd say with a big grin.

The moment we got into the house Ken and I would head back into the kitchen. I'd grab a Coke from the fridge and sit in a chair at the table. Ken would shake his finger at me in a *don't you dare tell your mother* kind of way and I would burst out laughing and shoot Coke out of my nose.

Mom would look over at me and then at Ken. He'd start laughing and just sit there saying, "What?" I'd follow with, "Honest, Mom, he didn't let me drive." Ken would look at me again and I would spit Coke all over the table as my gut exploded into fits of laughter.

Mom would say to Dad, "Would you tell this foolish bastard that it's dangerous letting the boys drive?"

Dad would just look over at Ken and grin.

Rick and Ken also got to drive with Ken, but I think I got to drive the most just because I was the youngest.

Rick, Ken, and I were very lucky to be born into a loving and caring family. Sure, Dad worked too much. But he had no choice. He was busy holding down as many as three jobs. He was a truck mechanic at Direct Winters Transport, he had opened Commercial Auto Electric, and for five years he drove a cab in his spare time. Mom was always busy taking care of – more like putting up with – us three boys.

But now, happy as our childhood was, it was taking a crisis to pull the family back together.

7

THE WAITING GAME

Later that morning we became acquainted with the ICU waiting room on the fifth floor. It had twenty-five or thirty chairs. There were seats lined up along the walls as well as in the middle. A nurse, or someone who looked like one, was seated at a desk where you entered. You were supposed to sign in and out as you passed by. I guess this was so that the doctors or pastors could find you if they needed you. There was a pay phone and a house phone just inside the door.

Kathryn was outside the waiting room talking to a bunch of people. One of the guys had his arm in a sling and a large, vertical cut on his forehead. I assumed these were the guys who were with Rick when the accident went down, but I was too tired to ask or care. I slid down in my chair and lay my head against the wall, closing my eyes for the first time in a very long time.

Everything seemed so surreal: this place, these people, these sights, this whole situation. How could this be happening to us? To Rick? I had seen Rick get his ass in a wringer more times than I could count, but he always pulled through, whatever the situation. Good luck this time, pal, I thought to myself. You're gonna need a miracle.

My thoughts drifted to my daughter, Hailey. I wondered what she was doing at that moment. Probably what any six year old does when she's with her grandmother: not much.

What would I do if she was the one lying there with a big plastic bolt sticking out of her head?

Click, besheeeh, click, besheeeh.

Don't think that.

What if Rick doesn't make it through this? What will my parents do? But he's going to be okay. Yeah, right.

My mind moved from Hailey to Cathy. It wasn't just Mom and Rick that I hadn't really connected with lately. Cathy and I had been a million miles apart, too. I guess it was something that happens to all couples at one point or another.

Cathy is without doubt the most patient and understanding woman on the planet. Hell, she agreed to marry me. And she agreed to get married in Jamaica on the beach, when I knew what she really wanted was a big flashy wedding. Just like the many that cost tens of thousands of dollars and end in divorce. That's something I could never figure out. People spend all that money on weddings and invite people they haven't seen in years and some they don't even like. It seemed to me that weddings were too often more for the parents of the bride and groom than for the bride and groom.

So on April 6, 1986, off to Jamaica we flew. We landed in Montego Bay and had an hour-and-a-half bus ride to our resort in Runway Bay. Soon after fighting off the baggage handlers at the airport, we boarded our rickety bus and began our trip to the resort.

A short while into our trip a girl working for the tour operator opened a cooler and began offering rum punch to all the people on the bus. She then broke out the Red Stripe beer and asked if anyone was interested in a beer drinking contest. Of course, my hand was the first up. As a few other hands went up, I looked around, checking out my competition. By the looks of things, I was in good shape.

Four or five of us guys opened our stubby Red Stripes and got "at the ready." When the girl at the front said GO, we all started to chug. I thought I was doing pretty well until I heard a very loud *ahhh* followed by a loud belch. I stopped drinking and looked around to see who the scoundrel was who had kicked my ass. It was a blond guy a couple seats in front of us. While he was still smiling proudly, I said to him, "Hey what are you doing tomorrow night at 6?"

"Hell, I don't know – why?"

"Well, I'm getting married – you wanna be my best man?"

The guy looked at his wife, shrugged his shoulders, and said, "Sure, why not?"

Cathy then looked at his wife and said, "Well, if he's going to be the best man, you might as well be the maid of honor."

The wife of my best man – and I didn't have a clue what his name was – smiled at Cathy and said, "Sure, that sounds great."

– – –

I thought of a conversation I once had with our good friend Peter Wright. Peter was an instructor with us at the Porsche Advanced Driving School. I don't know how it started, but we got talking about death. I do know that it was after a night of partying with all the other instructors and students at a driving school somewhere.

I told Peter I wanted to live forever but if it should all end tomorrow, that would be fine. Not that I wanted it to end. The point was that I was very content with my life. Peter said he felt the same way.

I wondered if Rick felt that way, too. I believed so, or more accurately, hoped so.

Rick had been more focused on his racing career than anyone else I had ever met. He pursued his dream ... period. Not only did his whole life revolve around race cars, his whole being did. To the point where he had ended more than one long-term relationship. There's some kind of mystique about dating a race-car driver for a lot of women. Then reality sets in. They realize that there is only one thing that matters in life and it's not food, rent, or Freedom 55. It's racing.

I was sure that if Rick could have woken up at that moment he wouldn't have changed a thing in his life. Not if it meant having to lead a different life.

I lifted my head, opened my eyes, and looked around the room. It was very quiet. Not many people were talking and those who were, were speaking in a whisper. All of the people in there had the same look in their eyes: confusion, frustration, despair, helplessness, hope, all rolled into one. Is that possible? Is there such an emotion?

A woman who looked to be in her early sixties came into the room. She seemed to know everyone – the local socialite, I thought. I heard her tell someone that she used to be a nurse at this very hospital. She was busy giving directions, advice, and whatever else anyone needed. She didn't hesitate to take anyone by the arm and lead them to wherever they needed to go. Her name was Sheila and she was there with her elderly mother, who was also in the ICU.

Over in the corner someone was curled up on a pile of coats. Boy, girl, man, woman? I couldn't tell. I wondered if their sleep was peaceful. Sleep, I needed some sleep. I wished I could just close my eyes and go to sleep. I had been up for about twenty-nine hours.

It was time to get back to the ICU. I took a deep breath, stood up, stretched, and exhaled deeply as I walked toward the far door so I didn't have to walk past the crowd in the hall.

It was about 10 a.m. and there was no change back at Rick's bed. No change in my parents' faces or in Cathy's either. Just the same blank look that they all had the last time I saw them. How did my face look? I wondered.

As for Rick, *click, besheeeh, click, besheeeh* pretty much said it all.

"Have any doctors been around?" I asked. Everyone quietly shook their head no. As we stood there, helplessly, Mom whispered to me, "Who is Constance Buck?"

"Who?"

"Constance Buck is the name the nurses have as an emergency contact," she said.

"Who the hell knows," I replied. "I'm sure we'll find out sometime soon. Till then I'll have them change the name to you guys and us."

— — —

The trauma team had six members. They advanced on us dressed in the usual drab hospital garb.

A Dr. Michael Chang identified himself as Rick's trauma leader and then introduced the rest of the team along with their areas of expertise. They included an orthopedic surgeon, an internist, a general surgeon, a neurosurgeon, and a couple of medical students from Wake Forest University.

Dr. Amy Olson stood out because she was the only woman in the group. She was the general surgeon. I wondered how old she was. Late twenties, early thirties, maybe. In fact, all of them looked so young. Perhaps the fact that the hospital was affiliated with the university had something to do with it.

The ICU remained clean, calm, and quiet. Everyone in there was working away slowly, but with purpose. The walls were gray and the stone floor shiny. The drapes over the windows were drab. And the sheets covering the dozen or so sleeping souls were white and plain. The silence of the room was broken by the steady beeps and the clicking of heels. And of course the ghostly, methodic, ever-present *click, besheeeh, click, besheeeh.*

"Well, I will start at the beginning," Dr. Chang said. "Please do not hesitate to stop me if you have any questions along the way. First thing I have to tell you is that Rick is very sick."

Sick, he's not sick, he's fucked up, I thought.

"Rick arrived yesterday at around four o'clock in the afternoon. The entire team was ready and waiting for him as we were noti-fied by the air ambulance that they were on their way with him. The first thing we did was make sure he was stable and then we began to determine the extent of his injuries.

"He has an open fracture of his right ankle and a badly broken left hip. As you have probably noticed, he has a number of cuts and severe bruising. Rick also has a closed-head injury, which is what we're most concerned about. All of the other injuries we know we can fix. Broken bones can be dealt with. With head injuries it is really a waiting game."

"So what exactly is his head injury?" I asked, not really wanting to hear the answer.

"He has a subdural hematoma, which is sort of a blood clot between two layers of the brain. That's what the ICP bolt is for. It will monitor his internal cranial pressure. That's the pressure inside his head. As his brain begins to swell, we can see it up there on the monitor. Right now his pressure is fairly steady at around twenty-five. Twenty-five is high, though. We would like to see it lower."

"So twenty-five is at the high end of the scale?" Mom asked.

"If you had a moderate headache, your ICP would be somewhere around five or six. If that number gets up to sixty, it can be fatal. At sixty, the pressure in your head is greater than your blood pressure. At that point, your heart can't pump blood up into your head. So as you can see, twenty-five is not good, but we really don't want to see it in the forties or fifties."

Dr. Chang went on to say that the brain would go through the greatest amount of swelling in the first seventy-two hours from the time of the injury.

"What will you do if the ICP numbers start to climb? Is there anything you can do to relieve the pressure?" I asked.

Cathy reached over and took my hand without looking away from Dr. Chang. Her eyes were locked on Dr. Chang, just as Mom and Dad's were. I knew at that moment that she wished I had not asked that question.

Even though we had been a little distant lately, our connection was deep and well rooted. Roots that had had twenty years to sink into the ground, that would keep us firmly planted through the worst of storms.

"Well, we have a few options," began Dr. Chang. "We can drill a hole in his skull and alleviate the pressure. But if it gets to that point, you will have some very difficult decisions to make. There comes a time when you have to consider quality of life over life itself."

Everything went ghostly silent. My mother leaned her head on my father's shoulder, covering her mouth with one hand. Her eyes were open and fixed on Dr. Chang.

"Is that it?" I asked.

"No," Dr. Olson replied. "When Rick was in the CAT scan yesterday, when he first got here, he had a grand mal seizure."

"A grand mal seizure?" I asked.

"It's a very serious seizure," Cathy said, looking up at me for the first time since the team had come into the room.

"That's right, a really serious seizure. Luckily he had it while he was in the CAT scan and we were there with him."

"So what happens during these seizures?" I asked.

"Well, it's sort of like an electrical storm inside his brain. The main issue is that he aspirated."

"Aspirated?" I asked.

"He threw up, then inhaled it," Cathy said.

"Yes, that's right," Dr. Olson said. "He was very lucky that we were right there at his side. If it had happened while he was still trapped in the truck, it would have been bad. Because it happened here in the hospital, we were able to intubate him right away."

"Intubate?" I asked.

"Clear his airway," Cathy said. Dr. Olson looked her way and nodded.

"So if he aspirated, does that mean that he may have gone some time without oxygen?" I said to no one in particular.

"Yes, that is always a risk," Dr. Olson responded quietly. "But I was there the entire time, from the time the seizure began to when it finished. We intubated him right away. Of course there is no way of knowing for sure if there was any oxygen depletion. But we're pretty confident at this point that there wasn't."

"Anything else?" I asked.

"Yes," Dr. Chang said. "When a person aspirates, their lungs fill with stomach content. This creates all kinds of problems. First, the stomach acids burn the interior of the lungs. The interior of the lungs is a very sterile place. With the stomach contents in there, there is a high risk of infection. Within the next day or so pneumonia will set in. This will bring high fevers along with the normal challenges that come along with the illness."

"So now what?" I asked.

"Sit back and wait. Try not to watch too much TV," Dr. Chang said.

"TV?" I was confused.

Dr. Chang shifted his eyes from me to the monitor above Rick's bed.

"The gauges and monitors – try not to watch them too much. The numbers can fluctuate a lot and can cause you all kinds of undue stress. Rick is very sick. He has a long, long road ahead of him. He has been here for almost twenty-four hours. The next forty-eight will be telling."

Dr. Olson was on next. "Please know that he is in the best hands possible. I can assure you of that."

I needed to be strong. I could not break down in front of anyone.

"We don't know for sure, but we think that a person in a coma can recognize familiar sounds and voices," Dr. Olson continued. "Talking to him will certainly not do any harm. It will be good for him to hear you. So by all means, talk to him as much as you like."

"We'll be back often," Dr. Chang said as he looked around at each one of us in a timed and practiced manner. "If you need anything, anything at all, just ask." He and his gang all curled up the corners of their mouths at the same time.

"Thank you," Mom said as the group turned and walked toward to two big doors of the ICU.

— — —

"It's F. David Stone. He wants to talk to you."

I turned around to see Kathryn. I guess I hadn't heard the phone ring. I had been standing in the same spot as when the medical team had left, beside Rick's bed. Had I been standing here for five minutes? Or five hours?

"Who?"

"F. David Stone. You know – the journalist." I walked over to the nurses' desk and picked up the phone. I took a deep breath. "Hello?"

"Is this Chris?"

"Yeah," I replied softly.

"Chris, this is David Stone from Kelly Moss Racing."

It was not F. David Stone – different guy, I thought as I looked over at Kathryn. I didn't know David, but I did know that he and Rick were very close. Kelly Moss Racing was one of the most successful Porsche racing teams in North America. David was the team owner. Rick had become good friends with him and had spoken about him many times. They were competitors as well as teammates.

"Price Cobb called me and told me about Rick's accident," David continued.

Price is without doubt one of the most respected Porsche race-car drivers in the world. His list of accomplishments is impressive, to say the least. He won races in everything he drove. He was the winner of the Porsche World Cup and was the 1990 24 Hours of LeMans champion.

"What can you tell me? What's going on? How's Rick?" David asked, all in one breath.

I tried to tell him about Rick's situation the best I could. I probably talked straight for three or four minutes. After I finished there was silence on both ends of the phone.

"Chris, I don't have a lot of friends in this world, but I consider Rick to be one of my very best. He's always been someone I can go to for advice. Now I know you and the family probably don't want anyone around and I can understand that. But I would really like to come down and see him. I understand if the answer is no."

"David, you are more than welcome," I said. "Come whenever you like and stay as long as you want."

I gave him my number and told him to find one of us first before coming in to see Rick.

His was the first of hundreds of phone calls that we took and made over the next few months. I knew Rick had a lot of friends, but I soon found out just how many.

— — —

It was time for my parents to leave the ICU again. They couldn't stay long before having to get out and regain their composure. As hard as this whole thing was on Cathy and me, we couldn't begin to imagine the pain they were feeling.

But we needed a break, too. As we walked around the corner toward the waiting room, we saw them talking to Kathryn and three guys, the ones who were with Rick when this nightmare began. They were John, Bill, and Rob. Rob had been traveling in the truck with Rick, and John and Bill had been following behind in a Mustang.

To this point Mom and Dad were present, physically. But they seemed to be in some faraway place emotionally. They hadn't really said too much. The enormity of the whole situation was still sinking in. They would be there at the start of conversations and then would simply disappear, at times back into the ICU to be with Rick and at others back into the ICU waiting room.

I remembered seeing Rob in the waiting room earlier. He was the one whose arm was in a sling. I asked him if he could tell me about the accident.

"Sure, but I don't know how much I can tell you because I was sleeping when it all started. All I remember is that it got really noisy, really fast. When I looked up, I saw cars and trucks everywhere. I knew for sure we weren't going to be able to stop in time."

"What was Rick doing?" I asked.

"He was fighting like hell. He never gave up. But there wasn't much he could do. There wasn't much anyone could have done." Rob looked blankly toward the ceiling and sighed. "That's about all I remember. That's when they got me out of the truck and took me away. I told them I didn't want to go. I wanted to stay and make sure Rick was going to be okay. They told me they couldn't wait for the rescue team to get Rick out of the truck. They wanted to get me to the hospital right away to check me out. So they put me in the ambulance and took me straight here. I have a dislocated shoulder, a broken collar bone, and a fractured skull."

"Where?" I asked referring to his skull fracture. He looked pretty good for a guy with a broken head.

"Right here," he said and pointed to a large gash on his forehead with stitches in it.

I was concerned about Bill because he didn't sound very good when I spoke to him at the crash site a day earlier. I found out later that he had held Rick's hand as the emergency crew cut him out of the wreckage.

Bill seemed to be off in some other land. "We crested the hill and almost crashed into the mess ourselves," he said, giving us his version of the events. "It took us a minute to realize that it was Rick and Rob. We jumped out of the car and ran to the truck. It was jammed under the back of a tractor-trailer and the roof had been sheared clean off. I jumped up on the truck and looked down inside. First, I saw Rob. He was moving around, covered in blood, and said, 'Get me the fuck out of here.' Then I saw Rick. He didn't look good. There was smoke and the guy driving the truck that they had hit ran and got a fire extinguisher and put the fire out that was under the hood."

Bill took a moment to catch his breath. "I didn't know what to do," he continued. "Luckily the emergency team arrived right away. They started to work on Rob and after they got him out they started on Rick. I stayed the entire time."

I had heard enough. I had to sit down somewhere. I headed slowly for the waiting room. I didn't realize it at the time, but I had just walked away from Bill without saying a word. I found a corner and sat in a chair, twisting my back toward the door so no one would notice me.

8
CRACKING ARMOR

We had been at the hospital for four or five hours now, though it seemed like a lot more. Someone suggested we should make some arrangements for accommodations and food. I remembered seeing an advertisement in the elevator for a hotel nearby called the Hawthorne Inn. I called and booked two rooms.

Lunch at Cagney's, a restaurant within view of the hospital, was very quiet and very good, though the parking sucked. The hospital looked even more spectacular from this vantage point.

I was amazed by how friendly and helpful everyone was. Not just at the restaurant, but everywhere we had been. We were being introduced to southern hospitality.

The girl at the checkout gave us directions to the hotel and we walked outside into the fresh, mild January air.

We turned left out of the parking lot and left again at the first light onto the entrance ramp for the freeway. As the road turned to the right, the lane ended and we were forced to merge into traffic at about twenty miles per hour. Cars were doing their best to let us in, hitting the brakes and jockeying for position.

"This is bullshit." I looked into my left-hand mirror to try and see where I could squeeze into traffic. I looked over at Cathy. "This is without a doubt the shortest entrance ramp I have ever seen."

She shook her head and repeated my sentiment: "It's bullshit."

"If we were driving a truck, there is no way we could merge safely," my father observed.

"It's bullshit," I replied.

We learned later that this corner kept the hospital in business. North Carolina has the shortest entrance and exit ramps on the continent. It was almost as if the traffic engineers were afraid of running out of land. I wondered if this had had anything to do with Rick's accident. At this point none of us had given any thought to how the accident had happened.

The Hawthorne was a nice hotel. It had four or five stories and about a hundred and fifty rooms, I guessed. As I walked up to the counter to register I asked if they had any special rates for families visiting the hospital. The girl behind the counter replied, "We sure do – we're owned by the hospital."

"The hospital owns this hotel?" I asked.

"Yep, they sure do. The hospital bought the hotel about five years ago. Over fifty percent of our business is hospital related."

"That's cool," I whispered.

— — —

We had probably been away from the hospital for about two or three hours. The drive back took only a few minutes and was uneventful, except for the highway ramp.

I'm not sure what I expected when we got back. Did I expect Rick to be awake and ready to chat? Did I expect him to be dead? The answer to both questions was yes. I had spent my time away from the hospital trying to prepare myself for whatever might come our way.

As we approached Rick's bed it was obvious that there had been no change. I wasn't sure if this was a good thing or a bad thing. His ICP pressure was still around twenty-five. His eyes were closed peacefully. His hands lay perfectly by his side. And his chest rose and sank in unison with *click besheeeh, click besheeeh*. He looked dead. And except for the *click besheeeh* machine, he was.

One of the nurses came over and introduced herself as Shirley. A tall guy with a moustache walked over and looked at the respirator. He looked familiar, but I knew I had never seen him before.

He adjusted a couple of knobs on the respirator and left without saying a word.

Shirley came over and quietly told us that she needed to suction Rick.

"Suction?" I asked.

"Yes, I have to suction his lungs," she said.

We thought she would ask us to leave and then would pull the blind around Rick's bed, but she didn't. So like an idiot I stood and watched as she slowly inserted a tube into one of the other tubes in Rick's mouth. Without warning, his whole body lurched upward. It appeared that every muscle in his body had suddenly gone full flex. His left leg, the one in traction, tried to straighten itself from its resting forty-five-degree bend. His right foot headed for the ceiling. His chin reached for the head of the bed and his back arched high. While all this was happening, his mouth opened as if gasping for air.

This was the first movement from Rick we'd seen since we got to the hospital. We stood there, frozen. My eyes quickly scanned over to the "TV." All I saw was 45 flashing on the ICP screen, then 55. Sixty was a fatal number, we had been told. I felt the power of an Evander Hollyfield right hook through the center of my chest. Cathy, Mom, and Dad were staring at Rick, their mouths half open and their eyes wide open. I don't think anyone else had noticed the monitor. I looked back at the nurse, who was continuing the suction process as if nothing was wrong. The numbers subsided – 50, 45, 40. Just as I took my first breath in what seemed like an hour, *bang*, the numbers jumped to 55. Shirley was once again sending the tube deep down Rick's throat and Rick's body was once again surging.

I looked to see if Shirley noticed the monitor. She didn't seem to be interested in anything but completing her unpleasant task as quickly as possible. Finally she realized we were in the room. She looked at my mother. "Oh my god, I'm so sorry," she said as she saw the horror in all of our eyes. "I should have had you all leave for this. I know it's hard to watch, but he's okay."

"The ICP numbers?" I asked.

"Oh, don't worry. It's normal for the ICP numbers to spike when someone gets suctioned. The good news is that he won't remember a thing about any of this."

I was pretty sure Mom and Dad hadn't taken a breath in the few minutes they had been in the ICU. It was time for them to take a break. Hell, it was time for all of us to take a break. I smiled at everyone. "I won't be long," I said and headed out of the ICU.

All of the same people were in the waiting room as I walked past. I turned left and headed toward the elevator. I didn't know where I was going but I knew that I had to get the hell out of the ICU.

Back at Rick's bedside, after about thirty minutes of wandering the halls, I realized it was getting late. Visiting hours were almost over, one of the nurses told us. "You are welcome to stay if you wish, but it might be a good idea for you to go and get some sleep." She assured us that they would all be there all night and would do whatever they could to keep Rick as comfortable as possible.

The first thing that came to mind as I unlocked the car door was to find a store that sold beer. I was definitely ready for a beer. Once again I cursed the entrance ramp as I merged into traffic. Nobody said a word from the time we left till the time we got to the hotel after stopping off and buying a twelve pack. We stood in the hallway outside our rooms. My parents' room was two doors down from ours. We split the beer. I snapped one open and took a long drink. We didn't talk much. None of us knew what to say. As we opened the door to our room, Mom looked at us and said, "We love you both."

"We love you, too," Cathy replied.

We made arrangements to meet in the morning, smiled at each other the best we could, and walked into our rooms.

I sat on the bed and looked at Cathy. We hadn't really talked to each other since this whole episode began, some thirty hours ago. I still didn't feel like talking. I could tell that Cathy understood.

We had been out of touch with the world for a long time. We knew there were a whole lot of people at Daytona, and elsewhere, who would be very concerned. I picked up the phone and dialed our voicemail at home. "Your mailbox is full. You have thirty-five new messages," the automated voice said. It took me a good five or seven minutes to get through all of the messages. As I made notes Cathy sat quietly clicking through the TV channels.

There were a couple of messages from Stephen Goodbody and

Trish Caughill, who run The Leasing Formula, an auto-leasing business, in Markham, Ontario. They were great friends. They had always made sure we had something to drive, even during the times when no one else would give us credit. They are two of the most genuine people I know. Stephen had traveled to Daytona this year to watch Rick and some of the Porsche teams compete. Stephen left his hotel number and asked me to give him a call when I had time.

"Hey, ya fat bastard," I said when I got him on the line. That's what I always called him. I knew if I addressed him any other way, he would have realized that things were not going well.

"So what's going on up there?" Stephen asked. "How is he?"

"Well, he's not very good."

Stephen went dead quiet and as I ran through Rick's injuries I could hear his breathing getting deeper. I asked him what he had heard down there in Daytona.

"Things are very quiet here," he said. "The only thing everyone is talking about is the accident. I went for dinner with Glynn and Patti and some of the Porsche Club people. They're devastated. I can tell you that no one down here is much interested in the race."

"Yeah," I said, swallowing hard.

I couldn't break down in front of Cathy. I stared straight ahead and didn't look at her.

"I saw Scott Harrington," Stephen said. "He wishes you well."

Scott was an Indy Car driver I had worked with on a few occasions. He was in Daytona driving a Camaro for one of the teams.

"If you see him tomorrow, tell him I said thanks."

"I will. One of the guys here was going around telling people that Rick lay in a hallway for ten hours before they would touch him. He said he had to prove that he had insurance before they would start working on him."

I could feel every muscle in my body tighten. Finally I had a chance to vent some of the frustration that had been building up over the last couple of days.

"You tell whoever said that that he must have been talking to Rick because the only one closer to the situation than us is Rick. So, maybe when I went to take a leak or something, Rick woke up and called the guy. The people here have been nothing but first class and Rick is getting the best care possible. In fact, the entire trauma team was assembled and waiting when the helicopter arrived."

"That son of a bitch ..."

"Tell him to keep his mouth shut, okay?"

"People!"

"Son of a bitch."

Stephen was dead quiet for a moment. "Will you call me if anything changes?"

"Yeah, I sure will."

— — —

I turned on the hot water tap first and then the cold. Once the temperature was right I locked the bathroom door. I had to wait till the shower was running so Cathy couldn't hear it lock. She would have thought it was a little strange for me to lock the door when I was having a shower. After all, we had been married for over twelve years.

I stepped into the shower and stood with my face in the direct line of fire. As I lowered my face and let the hot stream hit the top of my head, my shoulders started to hunch upward. Slowly at first, then more rapidly. My chest started heaving in sequence with my shoulders, and I started to sob.

My knees weakened and I soon found myself sitting on the shower floor. The water pulsated off the back of my neck as I sat with my knees pulled tight to my chest, my forehead resting on my knees. I sobbed so hard I had trouble catching my breath.

Cathy was already in bed when I came out of the bathroom. The room was dark except for the light from the TV. I got into bed and closed my eyes. I needed sleep. Cathy was awake. She took my hand in hers. We interlocked fingers. She didn't say a word, just squeezed my hand. I thought she had probably heard me.

"I love you," she whispered softly.

"Ditto."

9
THE LONG
ROAD AHEAD

The next morning, Saturday, we decided to have breakfast at the restaurant in the Hawthorne. At a table beside the window sat Rick's crew: Bill Hoeffle, Rob Collum, and crew chief Ted Bye. Ted is our uncle, the youngest of my father's six brothers. He worked as crew chief for Rick for several years and was a good one at that. He was one of the best I had ever worked with. He had an uncanny ability to remain level headed under pressure. He had taken time off his full-time job at John Deere in Welland, Ontario, to fly down to Daytona and once again head up Rick's Commercial Motorsports Daytona effort. Ted had been at Daytona waiting for Rick and the rest of the guys to arrive with the truck and trailer when he got the news of the accident. It was Ted's wife, Aunt Midge, who had called us when it happened.

Ted had arrived in Winston-Salem late the previous night. I knew the situation was much harder on him than he was letting on. I was glad he had come. We made arrangements with the guys to meet them later and left for the hospital.

The walk through the hospital lobby and down the long hallway toward the elevator was different from the morning before. This time we knew where we where going. We also knew what to expect, sort of. We knew what ICU 5B looked like. We knew what the ICU bed looked like. We knew what the ICU pod looked like. We knew what Rick looked like. Or did we?

Would the swelling and blistering be much worse, as Kathyrn had said? Would he still be in traction? Would they have cleaned out the dried blood in his mouth? Would he be better, or would he be worse? Would he still be there?

Click, besheeeh. Click, besheeeh. He was still there.

"He looks so much better than yesterday," Mom said.

It was true. The swelling in his face was down.

"How was he last night?" Dad asked a nurse. She told us Rick had had a comfortable night and that everything was normal.

Like all the others, this nurse seemed to spend just the right amount of time with the families before letting them know she wouldn't be far away if she was needed. Mom and Dad left for a break. Cathy and I checked our voicemail.

Once again our mailbox was full and once again I began the task of listening to friends and family who tried to sound calm as they expressed their concern for Rick and our family.

Cathy suddenly remembered that we could change the outgoing message whenever we wanted. "We can update his condition as it changes," she said. "At least people will be able to keep up with what's going on, even if they don't get to talk to us right away."

"That's a great idea. Glad I thought of it," I said with a feeble grin.

It didn't take long for people to figure out that updates were available in this way. Our phone line must have been the busiest in Canada. Most times our thirty-five-message limit was reached by the hour. Sometimes it was reached in half that time.

Message one, of many, went something like this: "Hi, this is Chris. If you are calling for either Cathy or myself, go ahead and leave a message. For all of you calling about Rick, today is Saturday, January 31, 9:30 a.m. I don't know what you know so I will start at the top. If you are calling this number then you obviously know about the accident."

I then recounted the details of the accident and Rick's injuries.

"Rick is on a respirator and is currently not breathing on his own. I can tell you all that he is in an amazing hospital. He is getting the best care humanly possible and if anything can be done for him, it can be done here. We will try to call as many of you back as possible, but it may take awhile so please bear with us. As soon as there are any changes, we will update this message."

So far I had done pretty well, but now my voice started to crack. I took a deep breath and finished as fast as I could. "It's going to be a long road ahead. We would like to thank all of you for your support. We have been and will continue to give Rick all of your messages. Stay strong and pray."

I left these messages when I could get a moment by myself, in this case at the phone on the first floor away from everyone. There was no way I could have left them in front of Cathy or my parents. As I dictated that front bulletin, two streams of tears dripped off my cheeks. I buried my head in the corner in case someone I knew walked by. I began to take deep, steady breaths. I wiped the tears from my face with my left sleeve, my right hand still on the receiver of the pay phone, my head against the wall. Finally, my heart rate began to fall. I clenched my teeth and straightened my back and stretched. Time to go back upstairs.

"The hospital administration wants to see us," Mom said as I approached her and the others outside the waiting room, which now included the rest of the crew.

"What do they need?"

"We're not sure. We met with a very nice girl. She needed some questions answered, but we couldn't answer them. Maybe you could go and see her?" She handed me a business card with the name Laurel Matthews in bold followed by an administrative title.

"She's down on the first floor," Dad added. "She's very nice."

I put the card in my shirt pocket and went into the unit to see Rick. A woman in the waiting room stuck her head into the ICU and called to us.

"The Bye family?"

"Yeah?"

"It's for you," she said, handing me the phone.

It was Ruedi Hafen, who operated Niagara Helicopters in Niagara Falls, Ontario.

"How's Ricky?" Ruedi asked in his heavy Swiss accent.

"He's pretty sick, Ruedi."

"He's going to be all right though, right Chris?"

"He's very sick," I said again. Ruedi didn't seem to realize the severity of the situation. I knew I had to be sensitive with him since he and Rick were best friends. I knew he would take any bad news very hard.

"Is he awake? Is he talking?"

"No, Ruedi. He's in a coma."

"Well, when will he wake up?"

"They don't know. It's kind of a waiting game."

"Will you call me the moment you know anything?"

"You bet," I said, letting him know he could get updates on our home number as well.

We spent the next few hours in and out of the ICU. When we weren't there, we were answering phone calls on both of the waiting room phones. When we were there, we were standing alone beside Rick's bed, not saying anything, just standing.

Click, besheeeh.

Click, besheeeh.

It was hypnotic.

I tried to comfort myself with the thought that if anyone could pull off a miracle, it was Rick.

— — —

The year was 1987 and Rick had just come off a successful 1986 racing season. He had finished fourth in the Rothmans Porsche Challenge race series. He was the highest "privateer" finisher, behind Bill Adam, Scott Goodyear, and Richard Spenard. Rick, along with his marketing and sponsorship manager, John Ross, began to look for sponsorship for the 1987 racing season. Rick had met the president of Reebok Canada through his day job at Heimrath Porsche. Rick and John put together a sponsorship package proposal and made arrangements to get together with Reebok Canada president Michael Sylvester. The presentation went well and after several weeks of not hearing back, Rick put a call into Michael. They agreed to meet again.

At the second meeting, Michael shared with Rick and John that he had three other proposals on his desk for the same race series and each one of them would cost less than half of theirs.

Rick calmly asked Michael why that was a problem.

Michael responded with the answer everyone expected. "Well, it's simple economics, half price for the same product. What's not to understand?"

Rick's turn. "Michael, some people buy ten-dollar running shoes at Wal-Mart – and others buy Reeboks."

Rick walked out of that office with a signed sponsorship contract worth ninety-five percent of Reebok Canada's advertising and marketing budget. Now that was miracle.

– – –

I also comforted myself with the thought that if anyone could pull off a miracle, it was the medical staff at this place.

Cathy walked in the room and grabbed my hand. "How ya doin'?"

I gave her the half smile that she was becoming familiar with. She returned the same smile, the one that means "as good as can be expected."

Uncle Ted came to Rick's bedside. I watched him as he looked at Rick for the first time. He curled up one corner of his mouth and said, as only he could say: "He looks like a Formula One car with all that shit hooked up to him."

I knew he was referring to all the hoses and wires and dials and gauges.

Time to go for a walk again. As I went down the hall past the waiting room, an elderly lady stuck her head out. She knew who I was because we were all in such close quarters. "Chris," she said, "some guy phoned the waiting room looking for you. I think he said his name was Hurley something? I told him you were here and he said he would call back."

– – –

Hurley was Hurley Haywood, deemed by many around the world to be the most successful sports car racer in history: five-time winner of the Rolex 24 Hours at Daytona, three-time winner of the 24 Hours of LeMans, and two-time winner of the famed 12 Hours of Sebring. Rick had worked with Hurley doing media launches for Porsche Cars North America and spoke of him frequently. He had a huge amount of respect for him.

Daytona. That's where Hurley was and that's where Rick should be.

In the late 1980s Hurley was a factory driver for Audi along with Hans Stuck in their Trans-Am effort at Mosport. There were no two names more famous than theirs when it came to sports car racing. They not only won just about every race that year, they embarrassed the competition. Their Audi quattros were unstoppable. Well, except for one thing: the wall on the outside of corner 3 at Mosport.

I was working for a Can-Am team at the time and the Trans-Am cars were also at Mosport that weekend. In fact, we were pitted right beside the Audi guys, and Hurley and I spent some time chatting. I was in awe of his and Hans's driving ability. They were just so dominant. You almost felt bad for every other driver and team in the field.

When the Trans-Am race got going on Sunday, Hurley and Hans took off and grabbed the lead just as they had done all year. Late in the race Hurley was lapping a car and the guy tried to get out of his way. The only problem was that the guy zigged when he should have zagged. He probably misjudged the speed at which the Audi was catching him. Hurley went high to the outside, and so did the other car. At 125 miles an hour it doesn't take much for things to go south in a big hurry.

The lapped car touched Hurley's car, sending it flying into the outside retaining wall, completely crushing the front of the car. Unfortunately, Hurley was crushed, too. It took the corner workers a long time to get him out of the car. His legs were mangled. One foot was hanging by nothing but tissue. He was transported to a hospital in Toronto. The doctors said there was nothing they could do to save his leg and they would have to amputate. Hurley was having none of that and insisted on being transported to Indianapolis to be cared for by the famed Indy Car doctor, Terry Trammel. Dr. Trammel saved his leg and Hurley not only would race again, he would eventually be able to ski again, too.

I wondered if Rick would pull through like Hurley.

Later I spoke to Hurley and told him to come down and see Rick if he wanted. We weren't really encouraging visitors, but for Hurley we would make an exception.

— — —

Back at the ICU, I checked in on Rick. He looked the same but that didn't mean he had lost his capacity to surprise us.

"Connie called. She says she's coming down," Cathy said. Connie was the mysterious Constance Buck who was the original emergency point of contact.

"Well, did anyone find out who she is?" I asked.

"Apparently she and Rick have been dating for some time."

"He's never mentioned her name to me."

"But that's not unusual for Rick," Mom said.

10

IT CAN'T GET ANY WORSE, CAN IT?

At around 5 p.m., later that Saturday, Cathy caught my eye and motioned for me to follow her out of the ICU. She took me by the arm and walked me around the corner.

"Amy Olson just left. They took Rick for another CAT scan."

"Why?"

"They think he had a stroke. His left side is paralyzed."

"And?"

"Well, he didn't have a stroke, but they found a large contusion on his right frontal lobe. Amy said that's probably what's causing much of the swelling and the paralysis."

I went straight to the nurses' desk. "Can you tell Dr. Olson or Dr. Chang that we want to see them when they get a minute?"

I have never been a big fan of hospitals – perhaps out of "racer's denial." In this case I was so focused on Rick and so much a part of his story that I hardly realized I was in one. Still, I was lucky to have Cathy with me. While waiting to talk to the doctors, I thought about another time when we were in a hospital together.

– – –

There are very few women on this earth who would put up with what Cathy has had to put up with. Like the times when I was at the track buying racing tires with our mortgage money. Or at the track while she sat at home and read. She certainly wasn't watching TV – our cable had been cut off.

I guess she has everything she has ever wanted. She has an amazing kid, our daughter, Hailey. I never wanted any kids. As far as I was concerned, kids would interfere with what I wanted in life. I thought about how much I loved Hailey, and how much I missed her. How I wished I could hug her right then. I thought about how we are best friends.

Unlike Cathy, my life was complete BH (our term for "Before Hailey"). I enjoyed my life with Cathy. I enjoyed it because I could be selfish. I could spend money racing and traveling. I enjoyed the time that Cathy and I spent down south scuba diving. I worried about how a child would limit my time with Cathy.

In late March 1992, as Cathy was in her eighth month of pregnancy with Hailey, I was in Victoria, British Columbia, launching the new Audi 90 and 100 to all of the Canadian Audi dealers. I was there with the guys I worked with in the Porsche Advanced Driving School: Len, Jud, Peter, and the others. We had been there for two weeks, staying at the Empress Hotel. On a rare day off Rick and I decided to go fishing along with a couple of the other guys. We didn't catch shit. But, we sure had fun. Rick sat there drinking his Diet Coke and killing himself laughing at the rest of us as we drank a few beers.

We had rented a small half-mile oval in Victoria to take people for what we call hot laps. We would strap in a group of salespeople into a car and take them around a makeshift road course that incorporated this oval. We were driving the new Audi S4, an awesome car with a 2.2 liter 5 cylinder turbo engine.

There are two types of people in your car during hot laps: ones who scream their heads off and have fun, and the others who don't say a word and hang on for dear life. The latter are more fun, because you know they're scared shitless.

Cathy was with my parents at Pearson International Airport in Toronto when I got back from this trip, on Sunday, April 5. She was as big as a house. The four of us decided to get something to eat on our way home.

When Cathy and I got to our home at 10 p.m., the only thing that I wanted to do was get reacquainted with my own bed. We had turned the TV off and I was drifting off to sleep when Cathy got up to go to the bathroom. I came to when I heard her calling my name.

"I think my water just broke," she said.

"Oh?" I replied, as I closed my eyes.

"Chris, my water broke!"

I attended those Lamaze classes, or whatever they're called. I just didn't pay much attention. I made something very clear to Cathy right from the beginning. If we decided we were going to start a family, there were two things I was not doing when it came to kids. One was the delivery room scene and the other was diapers. So whenever they brought out the videos, it was, later dude, I'm outta here.

I have always been a firm believer that society has been emasculating men for quite some time. This whole business about the delivery room was not for me. I still haven't figured out why men are supposed to be there. My father wasn't in the delivery room when I was born. In fact, I don't think he was even at the hospital.

It's ironic that there is so much pressure on men to be in the delivery room and divorce rates are at fifty percent. So many people talk about the only way to have a special bond with your child is by taking part in the delivery. I say bullshit. How many dads who were on the scene when their children were born now are nowhere in sight? And while we're on the topic, whatever happened to stags? When I was younger, the girls had a shower and the guys had a stag. Now the girls have a shower and the guys have a "stag and doe." What's up with that?

For the record, I love women and where they have come in the last several decades. I believe perhaps more than any guy on earth that men and women are equals. But that means equals. Many of my friends did not want to be in the delivery room. Sure, some truly felt it was an amazing experience, one they wouldn't have missed for anything. But then there are the others, those who have two very different versions of their children's birth, one for when their wives are present and another for when they're not. How come no one wants to admit this? Why is this topic such an elephant in the room that no one talks about? Why is it so politically incorrect to say as a guy that you don't want to be in the delivery room? Why do guys for the most part have no say in this matter?

If guys don't want to go into the delivery room, then they should have that choice. If they don't have that choice, then I guess it's their choice not to have it.

I had been to most of the pre-delivery appointments with Cathy. I had told Cathy's OB, Dr. Campagna, from the beginning that I wouldn't be going into the delivery room. I would be there to hold Cathy's hand through labor, but when it came time for the next step, it would be *exit stage left* for old chicken shit here.

No matter how much they told me otherwise, I knew I could be of no help whatsoever in there.

So at 11 p.m., with less than an hour of sleep, Cathy and I got into our car and drove the three kilometers to the hospital. Things were very calm there. They took Cathy away in a wheelchair while I got us registered. Then I went up to her room and began the long waiting process with her. Which was to be twenty-four hours long.

By six o'clock Monday night, Cathy was still in labor and the situation seemed to be getting a little tense. The doctor examined her one more time and was quite upset that the nurses had started Cathy pushing some time earlier. The baby's head was swollen and he believed it was from the pushing. Since Cathy's tailbone was somewhat in the way of the baby, it was starting to look like they would be doing a C section. The decision was made to take her into the delivery room.

I held her hand as she was rolled down the hallway and into the delivery room. I wasn't about to tell her so, but she really looked like shit. I figured her day was going bad enough.

We were there for what seemed like hours before I wondered why there was no sign of Dr. Campagna. I told Cathy I would be right back and went into the hall to look around.

"Have you seen Dr. Campagna?" I asked a nurse as she walked by.

"Yeah, I think he's in the doctor's lounge," she replied.

As I opened the door, I saw a pair of feet up on the coffee table. The doc was sitting there watching rock videos.

"Sooo, isn't this the part where one of us is supposed to do something?" I asked.

"Yeah," he said. "I'm just waiting for another doctor to get a second opinion."

"It's nice to see we're not dealing with any egos here," I said.

"There are only two things that matter right now, your wife and your baby," he said without lifting his eyes from the TV. I nodded and sat down beside him.

The decision under discussion was to do a C-section with the use of an epidural. I hated the thought of someone putting a needle into Cathy's spine, but it appeared there was no other choice. I was amazed at how tough Cathy had been. I couldn't believe that women wanted to do this to themselves. The only thing more confusing is the fact that most of them want to do it more than once.

When the decision was confirmed, I leaned down and kissed Cathy on the forehead and told her I wouldn't be far and that I loved her. Then I walked toward the doctor who was now in the scrub room.

"Doc, I will be right outside the door ... take care of her."

"Are you sure you won't stay?" he asked again.

"Quite."

"Can I ask why?" he said as he rinsed lather from his forearms.

I looked at his green smock and then down at his matching pants and down to his knee-high, bright yellow duck boots. Then my eyes slowly reversed their journey till our eyes met. "Because I don't know why you are wearing those boots, and I don't want to know," I replied and walked out the door.

I'm not sure how long I was out in the hall before a nurse brought out this little person wrapped in a blanket. The only thing showing was a tiny little face, and I mean tiny. I had never been much into babies, so I had never held one so small. In fact I had probably never held any baby before. The nurse reached out for me to take the little bundle. I put my arms out the way I had seen in the movies.

This little package opened her eyes and looked straight into mine. A smile came slowly to my face as she closed her eyes again. I was so glad she was a girl.

"Can I go back in and see Cathy?" I asked.

"You sure can," the nurse said, taking the baby from me.

"Hi," I said softly, as I approached the bed. "How are you doing?"

"I'm okay. How are you?"

"I'm good."

A nurse came over and placed the baby on Cathy.

"She's beautiful," Cathy said without looking up.

"Yeah," I replied as I saw pure contentment in her eyes.

— — —

I walked back into ICU 5B just as a team of nurses was unhooking Rick from his pod.

"What's going on?" I asked.

"We're just moving him to the room off to the side over there," one of the nurses said.

"Why?"

"We have a car accident victim coming in and we will need this bed for just a short while. Then we'll put him back."

"But you can't see him if he's in that room."

"He'll be fine. There are alarms that will tell us if anything starts to go wrong."

As Cathy and my parents and I stood outside the small room where they had put Rick, Dr. Olson approached. She was eating from a takeout container and looked down as she came closer. I was pissed. We had been waiting for several hours to see her and now she had the audacity to just walk by. As she passed us she looked up at me from the corner of her eye and grinned.

"You bitch," I thought, but couldn't keep myself from smiling.

Amy had the ability to bring a smile to my face and strengthen my spirit in these trying times. Once again, for some unknown reason, she brought me comfort.

I asked her about the paralysis.

"We thought Rick may have suffered from a stroke since he has no movement on his left side," she said.

"How do you know he has no movement when he's in a coma?"

"We stick needles into the bottom of his feet. Even people in comas respond to that."

She went on to say that the contusion on the right frontal lobe of his brain was causing his brain to swell, and this was what was probably causing the paralysis.

"How long will it last?" I knew it was a dumb question as soon as I asked it.

"We don't really know." Dr. Olson was always honest with us, even when we may have not wanted her to be. But she always softened the news with her caring attitude.

I looked into the room. Rick just lay there, lifeless, motionless.

Click, besheeeh.

Click, besheeeh.

I thought about how Rick had done everything he had ever wanted. He has raced Porsches at such places as Kyalamy, South Africa. He had finished, twice, in the top fifteen of the Porsche Cup worldwide points championship. He had led a Busch Grand National race. He had never wanted anything else in life. He had never wanted what most people want. Such as a wife and a family. Such as retirement and financial security. Rick had always wanted to race, period. At times he had been criticized for his relentless pursuit of success in motorsport.

I knew Rick's life had changed dramatically over the past several months since he and Wendy split up.

Wendy's father – my business partner, Hank Franczak – had been an official in the Rothmans Porsche Turbo Cup Series. He knew first-hand Rick's total commitment to his sport. He had seen Rick work relentlessly from year to year. Hank understood the selfishness of a race-car driver. He knew that for Rick relationships were very much a distraction.

But he could also see that Wendy was happy when she was with Rick. The two of them seemed to be very much in love. Sure, she could have found someone who could have given her more financial security. She also could have found someone who mistreated her.

Those who didn't understand Rick may have wondered why Wendy stuck around so long. Those who did understand him knew why. Rick was a very caring and giving person – if the giving didn't stand in his way of racing, that is. As long as anyone in his life understood that, everything would be fine. Rick never pretended to be anything other than what he was. He was a race-car driver. Always had been. Always would be. Maybe.

I was being questioned on a regular basis by a number of people about Rick's relationship with Kathryn. I never really knew how to answer, because I didn't really know anything. And I never wanted to. Rick and I never talked to each other about people's private lives, much less our own. If anyone ever lived by the sword, it was Rick. Would he die by the sword?

— — —

"Here are Rick's belongings," Laurel said, placing a few items on her desk. We had finally made it down to the first floor where Laurel was in charge of hospital administration. The four of us were sitting on the other side of the desk from her, not knowing what to expect.

"These are all the things that were in his pockets?" I asked.

"I'm sure there are more things in his truck if you want to go down to the junkyard and take a look," Laurel said. Looking at my mother, she continued, "But you probably don't need to go down there right now. I don't think that seeing the truck will do you any good. Do any of you know if Rick has insurance?"

"To be honest with you, Laurel, this is the first time we have even thought about it," I said. Rick wasn't the type to plan for anything. I was pretty sure the answer was no.

"Well," she said, "if he doesn't, and you can only afford twenty dollars a month, then that's what you'll pay. The financial end of this situation is the furthest thing from our minds right now, so let it be the furthest thing from yours."

We looked at Laurel, confused.

She continued, "We're pretty sure that the young Spanish kid in the bed next to Rick doesn't have any insurance. He's been in a coma here for three months. He was working on a farm. His parents were notified and they haven't been able to come here to see him. They can't afford to. Anyhow, he's getting the same care as everyone else in this hospital. The only thing that matters right now is to get Rick out of the woods. We'll worry about the money later."

Now we were really confused. This was the exact opposite of what we as Canadians had heard about the US health-care system: that if you needed hospital care in the US and didn't have insurance, they would wheel you out to the curb.

11
A BIG DAY

The trauma team was waiting for us when we entered the ICU on Sunday morning. It was not to give us good news. They began by saying they were concerned by how long Rick had had his respirator tube in. They wanted to put a permanent trach tube in, instead. They explained that the tube going down his throat could damage his vocal cords if it was in too long. With a trach tube, the tube would be below his vocal cords and he wouldn't have that problem when he got better.

"Yeah, but does that mean that you have to cut the front of his throat to install this tube?" I asked.

"Yes it does, but the scar fades very fast after we take it out," Amy replied.

We hung around for the balance of the morning. There wasn't anything new going on. Rick's condition had pretty much stabilized. His ICP numbers were still in the low twenties and there was still no response of any kind. By the middle of the afternoon we figured we would all go back to the hotel to get a little rest before the night shift.

When we got back to the hospital later that evening, the situation was very different. Drs. Chang and Olson told us the trauma team had decided it would be wise do the surgery on his pelvis the next day.

"How did we get here?" I asked. "Just a couple of hours ago you were ready to cut his throat and install a permanent trach."

Dr. Chang explained that after our meeting the orthopedic surgeons had said they wanted to deal with his hip issue. "The neuro guys obviously have to make sure that his head injuries are being taken care of properly," he said. "As a team we've decided to take him off of the medication and see how he does through the night. If he's stable, we'll do surgery tomorrow."

"Well, I guess that's good news," I said.

It's funny how lonely a place can be even when there are a lot of people around. ICU 5B hadn't changed much that Sunday evening, with that ever-present sense of calm urgency. How could anyone be calm in this place?

We stayed long into the night. Finally we decided it was time to go to the hotel and get some sleep. Tomorrow was going to be a big day.

— — —

The day of the Toronto Star 24 Hours of Mosport had finally come. Rick had called me the week of the race and asked if I wanted to join his Commercial Motorsport Porsche Team for the weekend as one of the team drivers. The year was 1992. I had just come off of a very successful 1991 racing season, and so had Rick. He and his Commercial Motorsport Race Team had just won the Firestone Firehawk Endurance Championship and were well on their way to winning another consecutive title. I had finished runner-up in the Esso Protec Formula 1600 Championship. I had not won the championship but had finished second to series champion Stephen Adams and ahead of a promising driver, Greg Moore, who was to become a Canadian Indy Car standout.

Stephen Adams was the toughest son of a bitch I had ever raced against. Finishing second to him was a bitter pill to swallow. I have a friend who always says that finishing second is like kissing your sister: it's okay but it's not the real thing. I will have to take his word for it, since I don't have a sister.

I knew Rick was going to be running two cars in the race and asked him who I would be teamed up with. He told me I would be driving the Motorplan Porsche. The driver lineup for the race would be Raymond David, Terry Betts, Rick, and me. I thought about it for about a nanosecond. "Hell, yeah," I said, trying not to sound too excited. But I *was* excited. I knew that Rick's team, headed up by Uncle Ted and with these co-drivers, would be considered a favorite to win.

Rick was an outstanding driver, with amazing car control. Raymond David was an insurance mogul who had been a driver with Rick's team for a couple of years. Terry Betts was a regular in the GM Players Challenge Series. I didn't know much about him but I knew he would be fast. I just hoped he would be reliable, and not crash, bringing the car home in one piece.

In endurance racing there are three types of drivers. First, the guys who have a lot of money but, as Rick would say, couldn't drive a nail through a block of butter. Second, the fast guys, who usually have no money. You know they'll be fast and since they have no cash they're not likely to crash. And third, the ones who bring money to the team and can also drive.

Raymond was in the third category. He had a very successful insurance business in Montreal and commuted to the racetrack in his Jet Ranger helicopter. He took his racing as seriously as his business. He worked hard at being fast, and fast he was. He was just a great teammate and an all round good guy – one of those guys that people in the racing business love to talk about. A lot of them complained that he had too much money, but they obviously didn't know Ray. At least not the way we knew him.

After we qualified, we had a team meeting to discuss race strategy. We all decided Ray would start.

When the green flag dropped, at 1 p.m. on Saturday, Ray stormed off, leading some fifty other cars down the front straight of Mosport and down into corner 1. The rest of our team, fifty strong, watched as we settled into what would be a very long day.

Ray's first stint was flawless, as usual. After approximately one hour and forty-five minutes Ray brought the Porsche 944 S2 onto pit lane for a driver change, tires, and a full tank of fuel. Under a minute later, Rick stormed off, without losing the lead. After Rick, it was Terry's turn, and then, almost six hours after the green flag, it was time for me to strap in.

There is no way to describe the feeling of standing on the pit wall, with your driver's suit done up, your gloves and helmet on, waiting for your car to come into view. Terry brought the Porsche in, still in the lead. As the car came to a stop in our pit stall, the crew came to life.

One, two, three, four, five guys over the pit wall and a flurry of activity. By the time I jumped off of the pit wall and ran around the rear of the car, to the driver's side, Terry had the door open and the car was up in the air. I helped Terry get out of the car and he in turn helped me get in and get the belts on. The six-point safety harness is very difficult to do up with your helmet on. After I was strapped in tight, Terry connected the plug on the side of my helmet for my radio.

"There's some oil in corner 8, it's pretty slippery, be careful," he yelled. "The car's great." He slapped the top of my helmet, put up the safety net, and closed the door.

My eyes were totally focused on Jeff, who was at the front of the car with his arm straight out and his palm facing me. This meant just sit and relax until the crew finished their work. My hands were at nine and three on the steering wheel. I grabbed the shifter and made sure the car was in first gear. I clicked the button on the steering wheel for a radio check. "Loud and clear," said Ted on the other end of the radio. The car slammed to the ground with four fresh Firestones, the oil checked, a full tank of gas, and a clean windshield, all in under a minute.

Go, Go, Go, Ted yelled into my radio, as Jeff dropped his hand and stepped out of the way. The car started to roll as I released the clutch and pulled toward pit exit. "Be cool – we still have the lead," Ted's voice echoed in my helmet. I glanced in the mirror to see the entire crew watching as I left the pit lane. The light at the end of pit lane was green and I accelerated onto the front straight. As I headed down the long right-hand corner 1, the car was still getting up to speed.

Mosport is one of the greatest racetracks in North America. By this point, Rick and I had been racing there for more than fifteen years. As I slid out of corner 10 with my right foot firmly planted on the floor, just where a Porsche likes it, and onto the front straight to finish my first lap, I looked toward my pit. Rick was leaning over the pit wall and looking straight at me. He gave me one of his normal looks of concern as I flashed by at one hundred plus miles per hour.

We maintained the lead well into the night. At about 4 a.m., a half shaft broke. The car sat out on the track for about thirty minutes till a tow truck brought it back into the pits. Approximately five minutes later, the Motoplan Porsche was back into the race, with a new half shaft and a new driver – my turn once again. We had lost the lead while the car sat on the side of the track waiting for a caution lap. By sun-up, we had the lead again.

When the checkered flag dropped at 1 p.m. on Sunday afternoon, we had won by a large margin. When Ray brought the race car down pit lane after receiving the checkered flag, we were the proudest race team in the world. There we were all fifty or so of us, standing in pit lane, and every one of us reaching for the sky, fists clenched and pumping. As Rick, Ray, Terry, and I stood on the podium to receive our first-place trophy, I looked over at Cathy and Mom and Dad. We were all on top of the world.

The 24 hours of Mosport was really the first major race in which Rick and I were teammates. And we not only won, we kicked ass.

– – –

Monday morning we walked into the ICU with anticipation.

"He did great through the night," one of the nurses told us as we stood at Rick's bedside.

As she was talking, we noticed that his ICP bolt had been removed and the hole it left was covered with a large wrap that completely covered his head.

Amy Olson came into the ICU and walked straight to Rick's bed-side with her head buried in a chart, as usual. She stopped without looking up.

"After watching Rick all night, we've decided that he is ready for surgery," she said. "It's scheduled for 1 p.m. The team will meet with you shortly and let you know what's going to happen."

They approached as they always did. A team. A team walking with a purpose. Most of them head down looking intently at their charts. The others talking casually about the local bars or restaurants they had been to the night before. Led, as usual, by the young and impres-sive Dr. Michael Chang.

"Okay, it looks like he is ready," Dr. Chang said. "Rick had a very good night and we've decided today is the best day for his surgery. His ICP numbers were very low throughout the night and as you can

The start of a good thing: Cathy and me on our wedding day in Jamaica in 1986.

Rick Bye (left) and Raymond David being interviewed by automotive TV show host Tom Hnatiw.

Moment of victory: Rick (left), Richard Spenard, David Tennyson, and Scott Goodyear on the victory podium after a Rothmans Porsche Turbo Cup race at Mt. Tremblant, Quebec, in 1988.

The Porsche Advanced Driving School, 1989. Rick is in the front row, sixth from the left, and I am on his left.

Commercial Motorsport Porsche #21 wins the 24 Hours of Mosport in 1991. Drivers were Raymond David, Terry Betts, Rick, and me.

On victory podium: Stephen Adams, Greg Moore, and me at Shannonville Motorsport Park, 1991.

In victory lane: Rick (left) and teammate Raymond David enjoying another win, in 1991.

With my best friend: My daughter, Hailey, and me just before a race at Mosport, 1995.

Nothing sacred: Rick's Ford F350 Dually pickup truck is consigned to the junkyard the day after the crash.

With Cathy and friends
Nancy Price and Dianne Uppal
at one of our favorite bars,
near Las Vegas.

Rick walking to his Reebok
Porsche Turbo Cup car just
before a race in 1988.

Down time: Riding my Harley on
the way to the annual Laughlin
River Run, near Las Vegas.

Winners circle: With my daughter, Hailey, after a race in 1995.

Take a big breath: Yes, it is possible to relax before starting time.

Rick, Raymond David, and the Commercial Motorsport team enjoying another win on their way to the Firestone Firehawk Endurance Championship in 1991.

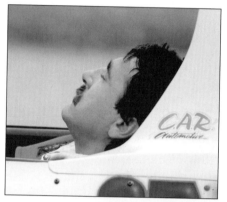

With Formula One racing star René Arnoux at the 2000 Beetle Cup race held at the Canadian F1 Grand Prix in Montreal.

With friend Jim Price in Oatman, Arizona, during the 2005 Laughlin River Run.

Checking the damage: Rick (bottom, right) examines his Reebok Porsche after a spectacular crash at Mosport in 1989.

The Brumos Racing Red Bull Porsche-powered Daytona Prototype driver lineup at the 2003 Rolex 24 Hours of Daytona: David Donohue (left), Mike Borkowski, Randy Pobst, and me.

Keeping in touch: Rick in the pit lane at Mt. Tremblant, Quebec, talking on the radio with his teammate in the race car.

With racing legends Brian Redman and Hurley Haywood, at the 2000 Beetle Cup in Montreal.

The Brumos Racing Porsche-powered Daytona Prototype in pit lane before the start of the 2003 Rolex 24 Hours of Daytona. We led in the first six hours before falling out of the race with mechanical problems.

Sweet moment: Giving Greg Moore a champagne shower along with Stephen Adams, on victory podium at Mosport in 1991.

The Commercial Motorsport Porsche 944 S2, which crashed at 2 a.m. during the 1992 24 Hours of Mosport.

Preparing for the start of the Mt. Tremblant race in 1995.

see, we removed the bolt this morning. As we said earlier, the first seventy-two hours are the most critical when it comes to head injuries. Rick has done amazingly well. We're all confident that today is the day to go in and fix that hip."

"Are you sure his head is okay and that he'll get through the surgery?" I asked.

"Look, Chris, there is nothing for sure in this situation," Dr. Chang said. "You will have to sign a release to allow us to do the surgery. Rick is still very sick and there's a chance he won't make it through the surgery. However, we think his chances are very good. If we didn't think he was ready, we wouldn't be going into this."

We trusted Dr. Chang. We had to.

He went on to explain that Rick would be brought into the OR around 12:30. He said we should go to the OR waiting room. They would call us from there with regular updates.

At precisely 1 p.m. the phone rang in the waiting room. It was just the four of us there. I answered the phone.

"Is this Mr. Bye?" the voice asked.

"Yes, it's Chris, Rick's brother."

"Chris, I am one of the OR nurses and I am calling from the OR. The doctors have just finished getting Rick ready for surgery and they are about to start soon. I will call you in a bit and let you know how things are going. Do you have any questions?"

"I guess not – we'll just wait to hear from you."

"Chris."

"Yeah?"

"He's in great hands."

"I know."

One hour later the phone brought us out of our books. It was the nurse again. "Rick is doing just fine," she said. "The doctors are starting to work on his hip. His vitals are good and everything is going just fine. Do you have any questions?"

Hour by hour, the calls came in. We got the final call at about 5 p.m.

"We're all done," one of the nurses said. "Rick will be taken straight back to the ICU, so you can go see him up there. He did just fine."

Rick looked pretty much the same. Dr. Olson came over to us.

"We have stopped the coma-inducing drugs and we are going to let him wake up when he's ready," she said.

"When will that be?" Mom asked.

"We can't say. It could be tonight, it could be tomorrow – we'll just have to wait and see."

Dr. Olson encouraged us to go get something to eat. "If he wakes up tonight, it's not going to be for a while," she said.

We heard what we wanted to hear, not what she had really said. We heard that Rick would be waking up that night and that we needed to go and eat so we could be there when he did. We all thought – or at least wanted to think – that we'd come back and he'd be sitting up in bed asking when he could go home.

We relaxed a little over dinner. We were looking forward to getting back to the hospital and getting the word that maybe we'd all get to go home later in the week. As we walked back into ICU 5B, we felt the first bit of hope in five days. For the first time since we arrived in Winston-Salem, we were letting our guard down.

Big mistake.

Rick showed movement for the first time, but not good movement. Convulsions, vibrating, and heavy, irregular breathing. He wasn't heaving, but almost. His skin was still stretched tight across the areas that were swollen, which was pretty much everywhere. He looked like a balloon full of water. He was covered in sweat, head to toe. His mind was not connected to his body. His body was not connected to his mind.

We just stood and stared, shocked, humbled, confused.

The trauma team came our way. "Rick came through surgery with flying colors but he's still very sick and has a long road ahead of him," Dr. Chang said. "He's going to need you all to be strong."

I've already reached down to my toes, I thought. Where is more strength going to come from?

"When do you think he will wake up?" I asked.

"Chris, we don't really know. It could be hours, days, weeks. We simply don't know."

Well, if you don't know, then just who does? I thought. In racing, everything has an answer, everything has a solution. Many times these answers are not simple or easy to find, but they are there.

How can anyone exist in a world where there are no answers? How can someone so obviously brilliant not have the answers? How can someone so brilliant accept not having the answers? In our world, Rick's and mine, if someone else was faster in qualifying, there was an answer why. The short answer was always the same: they were better than us. The long answer was to find out why they were faster and then make ourselves better than them. Never easy, but always doable. The fact that both of us worked until we found the answer was one of the reasons that we had been successful on the racetrack.

The convulsions got worse by the hour. Along with the convulsions came fever. And what a fever – it was steadily climbing, 101, 102, 103, 104. The higher the fever, the more severe the convulsions, with his skin stretched so tight it looked like it was about to split.

What will his life be like, what will our parents' life be like, what will my life be like? I wondered as I walked down the hall away from his room.

I knew it was selfish of me to wonder about my own future. The fact that my life had already changed dramatically was becoming more and more apparent with each passing day.

I sat and thought about how different my life had been than Rick's. The only thing we had in common was our racing lives, though we both also loved to have fun more than anyone I knew. Having fun was what I lived for and I wasn't having much of it right then.

– – –

It was the middle of the summer, 1979, and I had been racing for two years. When I was not spending my weekends at a racetrack somewhere I could be found riding my motorcycle with my friends from my other life, my biker life. A lot of racers never have a life away from the racetrack. Rick was one of them. His life was one dimensional and always had been. his friends at that time were his racing friends.

My biking brothers and I used to ride our bikes into northern Ontario, usually to the small town of Orillia. There would usually be five or six of us. My best friend, Jim, who now lives in Las Vegas, his brother, Gary, and our friend, Mike, would be there for sure and a few other guys would join us. Different guys on different weekends. The four of us were the core group.

We would leave St. Catharines or Niagara Falls on Friday afternoon and head north on the QEW highway. It was pretty much guaranteed that if we planned a bike trip, it would rain – at times so hard we had to park under an overpass along with a couple of dozen other bikers and wait it out. There were a couple of other guarantees when we all got together, too. One was that Mike would get in a fight with outsiders and the other was that Jim and Gary would fight like hell. They were brothers and it was just their way of relating.

It's strange how some brothers are like that and others get along just fine. Rick and I raced together and worked together and could just hang out. But this was not the case between me and my other brother, Ken. He and I used to fight like hell.

After arriving in Orillia we would check into some fleabag hotel. No Four Seasons for us, not on our budget. We would put four guys in a room. It sure wasn't pretty. We would sit in the room before going out and drink a few beers. By the time it came to head to the bar, it would be late. Off we would go to Champs, our favorite bar.

Once in the bar everyone would scatter. Champs was one of those bars where the music was too loud and there were way too many people. One of those bars where everyone was pushing and shoving and spilling drinks on everyone else. One of those bars that was great when you were nineteen – or, if you're Jim or me, no matter how old you are.

I have a bladder the size of a thimble and when I'm drinking beer, it seems to get even smaller.

On one of these visits I walked up to the urinal and as I stood there someone leaned into me. It was Jim. He came out with one of his usual lines, such as, "Man that water is cold" or "Is this where all the big dicks hang out?" If I heard those once I heard them a thousand times and every time I did, I laughed my ass off. Jim just has that knack of knowing how to make people laugh. He was the king when it came to funny.

There's not much to do when you are standing side by side, elbow to elbow, taking a leak. Just look at the wall and laugh. Or if you're Jim you look down at the guy beside you and laugh.

Jim gave me a tap with his elbow. He turned his head and looked down. Sticking out from the stall next to us was a shiny new white

Reebok, and guess who it belonged to? Yep, sure enough, it was Gary's. He had been showing off his new shoes before we went out.

Jim turned to the right at full stream. The stream hit its target, Gary's right shoe. If it was anyone else I would have been shocked, but because it was Jim, I started to laugh so hard I couldn't control myself. Gary's foot just stayed there for what seemed an eternity. Then, flash, it was gone.

"You son of a bitch," Gary screamed at full volume. There was no doubt in his mind who had just watered his new Reebok. There was a lot of crashing and banging in the stall. I finished as fast as I could and headed for the door. Jim was right behind me, knowing full well that Gary would come out swinging. We ran upstairs and across the bar so we would have a view of the restroom door.

Sure enough, the door flew open and there was Gary, red-faced and with fire coming out of his nostrils.

"He is some pissed," I said to Jim.

"Yeah ... especially his foot," Jim said as he and I curled up laughing. Gary was running around the bar crashing into just about everyone. I don't think I have ever seen anyone that furious.

"Come on, let's get the hell out of here before he finds us," I said.

We headed out onto the street to find another bar. After all of the bars closed, we headed back to our motel, hoping Gary was fast asleep. Not so lucky. In fact he wasn't even there.

"No problem," Jim said as he locked the motel room door and put on the safety latch. I laughed even harder than before. We opened another beer.

Bang, bang, bang on the hotel room door woke me up.

"Open the door, you bastards," Gary screamed. I looked over at Jim, who was totally out.

"Open this damn door," Gary screamed even louder.

"Okay bro, I'll open the door, but you know it wasn't me who watered your foot, right?"

"Just open door. I know who it was."

I walked over to the door and slowly took off the safety latch.

"Open this damn door," Gary screamed again.

"Bro, relax, I'm trying."

I finally got it open and jumped straight back into my bed,

preparing to watch World War Three. Gary came through the door and flew through the air, landing square on Jim. I was amazed at how quickly Jim came to life, immediately starting to laugh. Even when there was a mad man on top of him with murder in his eyes, Jim still managed to laugh.

"Yee haw, get him, Gary, come on pound him," I said, as I had no intention other than to stir the pot as much as possible. Fists were flying both inside and outside the blankets. People in the next room were banging on the walls. Gary was snarling and snapping like a pit bull.

Jim was laughing his ass off and since he was significantly bigger than Gary, he was pretty much in control. After about fifteen minutes, both brothers ran out of steam and the pace cooled off a little. I wasn't sure how long it had been since Gary had come flying through the door, but all was quiet and everyone passed out.

When I opened my eyes in the morning, the only thing I could think of was, Oh my god, what did I do to myself last night? My whole body hurt.

"Smells like piss in here," Jim mumbled.

I rolled over and start laughing so hard my head felt like it was about to explode. "Bro, don't make me laugh, my head is killing me," I yelled.

Jim just lay there laughing.

A quiet but undeniable "screw you" came from Gary's bed.

— — —

Over the next several days, things were fairly stable with Rick. But stable was not good. As the weekend approached, the fact that things were not any different was becoming tough to take. Just more sweating, convulsions, and high temperatures.

And a whole lot of nothing. Times when there was no movement, no eye movement, no limb movement, no head movement. And then back to those damn convulsions.

12
STATE OF NOTHINGNESS

The next few days were spent traveling between the hospital and the Hawthorne. The halls of the hospital remained green, the room at the Hawthorne remained comfortable, the people in Winston-Salem remained nice ... and other than his convulsions subsiding a little, Rick remained the same. Every day consisted of checking in on Rick to see if there was any change, returning phone messages, going for coffee breaks.

We spent our time simply waiting. When would Rick wake up? *Would* he wake up?

As the week went on, he began to look calm. Too calm, like the Spanish kid beside him, who had been in that kind of state for three months.

Driving a race car is, in a strange way, calm. Nothing and no one exists at the time. Just you and the car. I wondered if he was experiencing that kind of calm right now in his hospital bed. And if he was, was that okay?

The doctors told us Rick could probably start to breathe on his own and that the respirator was hooked up just for support. The more support he got, the easier all of this would be on him, they said. The week seemed to drag on into eternity. It was like one very long day that switched back and forth between light and dark.

– – –

I thought of standing at the pit wall at Mosport, with Rick flying by in the Commercial Motorsport Porsche.

I could see the side of the Porsche first as he came out of the last corner of the track and onto the pit straight. The front of the car grew rapidly as he accelerated toward me and the rest of the crew. I tightened the muscles of my neck as I prepared it to twist, as if being hit by right hook. The Porsche went flying by so fast that I couldn't see the numbers. As my head flew to the right, the Porsche belched out a fireball from the exhaust as Rick lifted the throttle, grabbed the next gear, and slammed the throttle back to the firewall. I tried to see into his eyes. The sunlight glared off the windscreen.

I knew Rick was unaware of anything around him. Just him, the race car, and the other cars on the track. Even so, maybe he was aware of me watching him, as I was always aware of him watching me. Actually, he was perhaps the only person in the world I was aware of when I was racing. Ted, our crew chief, of course was always at the pit wall and I could see him from inside the car. But when Rick was out at the pit wall, I always looked into his eyes as I screamed by, shifted, and blasted down the front straight.

– – –

When I walked back into the waiting room my mother was sitting talking to the socialite. Her name was Sheila Johnson. As I sat down, my mom looked over at me and said, "Chris, what is it exactly that Rick does for a living?"

"That's a good question," I replied.

– – –

Most of Rick's work had something to do with Porsches. It wasn't until 1988 that I was invited to be on the instructor team for the Porsche Advanced Driving School, and that's when the fun started. Rick was already on the team.

Being an instructor for Porsche was a feather in my cap that I was and will always be proud of. Unlike today, very few if any other manufacturers back then had a driving school. One thing was for sure, there was no other school in Canada or the US with an instructor lineup like Porsche's. The guys on this team had outstanding racing credentials. But more importantly, they knew how to have fun. And man, did we have fun.

We would party at night and work all day at a racetrack and then do it all over again the next day. And partying right along beside us would be Rick, Diet Coke in hand. Rick was the only one of the group smart enough not to drink. In fact, he has never drunk alcohol. We couldn't figure out how he managed to hang out with all of us and still not drink.

The schools were always held over the course of a weekend. We would fly into a city like Vancouver on a Thursday, head out to the track Friday morning for set-up, and then get ready for the Friday-night cocktail reception. The reception, held at the hotel where we were staying, was where the sixty or so students would come for their formal welcome. There would be between fifteen and twenty instructors.

At these events we instructors were expected to mingle and introduce ourselves to the guests. The invited guests were all new Porsche customers. I always looked forward to the receptions because we always met so many interesting people: airline executives, plastic surgeons, business tycoons, and rock stars, you name it. There were so many people with so many success stories.

Besides, there was always something really special about Porsche people. Some were excited, some were nervous. After mingling for a while we would tell our guests to make sure they got to bed good and early because they were in for a very busy day. Then we would head off to our favorite bar in the area, invariably with a couple of students in tow. We would stay out way too late and then have to get up way too early.

I remember it like it was yesterday. Hank Franczak – now my business partner – was our fearless leader. He would come into the breakfast room and sit down without saying a word. Then he would look around the room and take a head count. Eventually he would say, "You guys look like shit." Someone, usually Lenny, would come back with something like, "Yeah, looked in a mirror lately?"

After a breakfast of runny scrambled eggs and burnt bacon

we would head to the track to prepare for the students' arrival. Just as the ride from the airport the day before, the ride to the track would not end up a race, it would begin as one.

Speaking of the ride from the airport to the hotel, it was always one to look forward to, especially when we were in Vancouver. We knew it would be raining, just like always, when we landed there. And the locals would always say the same thing: "You should have been here last week. It was beautiful."

Regardless of the weather, Vancouver is one of the most beautiful cities in the world. And as far as the rain goes, it was a good thing. It would make the race from the airport to the Coquitlam Motor Inn much more exciting.

We usually started off with four or five rental cars and one minivan. We made sure we all rented front-wheel-drive V6 North American cars. You know, a Ford Taurus or a Pontiac Grand Prix. Our research had proven that if it was raining hard enough, and it would be, these cars had enough horsepower to maintain 120 kilometers per hour with their rear wheels locked solid.

Once we got up to speed on the highway, we would crank the handbrake on as hard as possible, at the same time slamming the throttle to the floor. The rear wheels would lock solid and the front tires would drag the car down the highway maintaining the given speed. There we were, four or five rental cars full of perfectly normal adults – well, okay, almost normal – racing bumper to bumper, passing each other and other cars with our rear wheels not turning.

People would pull up beside us blowing their horns pointing at the rear tires of our cars. Many would roll down their windows and wave frantically. We would all look straight ahead trying to keep a straight face. Then one of us would turn, smile, and wave. We wouldn't be able to hold it in any longer. We would burst out laughing.

You could bet your ass that Rick would be driving one of the cars. By the time we got to the hotel, the tires on the rental cars would be a square as the tires on Fred Flintstones' car. If you were unfortunate enough to be sitting in the back seat, you would swear your teeth were going to vibrate out.

"Great," someone would say, "We're going to have to ride in this thing all weekend."

As soon as we got checked into the hotel, the drill was always the same: off to Hank's room for a meeting. Hank loved meetings. He would have meetings to decide when the next meeting would be. And these meetings would always start with:

"Okay, where's Lenny?"

"On a beer run."

Then Hank would officially start the meeting. "Okay, you guys have got to lighten up on the rental cars. It's getting to the point where we can't rent cars anywhere in Canada. You guys have got to stop screwing around."

Just about then Lenny would walk into the room and start tossing beers to everyone.

"Oh, am I late?" Lenny would ask, looking at Hank with a straight face.

We would all burst out laughing. Hank would get pissed.

"Sorry, Dad," Lenny would say as he chugged his beer and let out a loud belch.

That would get us laughing like a bunch of school kids. What is it about a belch that makes guys laugh?

Hank would look straight at Lenny and say, "Sit down. Now listen up, guys. I'm serious."

Jud would lean over to Peter and say under his breath, "Good thing somebody is."

"Jud, you say something?" Hank would ask.

"No, Dad," the standard reply would come. Every one of us called him that. He was charged with the impossible task of trying to keep us in line.

"Meet in the lobby in one hour. We're going to the track to set up," Hank would say in his monotone voice.

"Does that mean this meeting is over?" someone would ask, laughing.

We would all grin at each other as we walked out of the room.

"And I suggest that you guys don't stay out all night. Get some rest. We have a lot of students this weekend."

"Yes, Dad," we would say in chorus.

We all knew that once the red wine started to flow, Hank would be just fine.

One hour later, the group of rental cars would pull out of the Coquitlam Motor Inn, throttles to the floor, handbrakes full on, as we headed for Westwood Motorsport Park. Hank would have his own car and lead the way out of the hotel parking lot. Of course, before he could say, "Take it easy on the rental cars," we would be screaming past him. We would look at him with a look of confusion on our faces and shrug our shoulders as we passed. Hank was usually with one of the girls from the travel agency or one of the Porsche executives. He would just look at us and shake his head.

Once at the track you never knew what might break out. It wasn't like we really planned for these things to happen, they just did.

On this particular trip the gate was locked. I don't remember who saw it first, but someone said, "Hey, look at that." "That" was a go-kart track we hadn't noticed before. And it had no fence around it.

The first thing I knew, Rick was saying, "Jump in" and a bunch of the guys got into his rental. Regan looked over at me and gave me a quick nod. I jumped into Regan's car and three others piled in. Rick's car disappeared over a crest as Regan stood on the gas and dropped the poor old Pontiac into drive at about five thousand rpm. *Screeech*, we were off.

Sailing over the hill we saw that Rick was already on the track doing practice laps. The track was about six inches wider than his car, but that didn't seem to bother him or anyone else. As Regan maneuvered through the gate, Peter Wright said, "Oh oh, here we go. This should be interesting." Regan pulled the car onto the track in front of Rick, who had already done a couple of laps. Everyone in our car was complaining about how Rick got to practice and we didn't. Rick stuck the nose of his car under the rear of our car as we entered the first corner.

"Go, Regan, go," we all screamed. Regan slammed the throttle to the floor and the race was on. Rick was all over us, left, right, left. No one seemed to think about the fact that the road was barely wide enough for one car let alone two. Regan was working the throttle, brakes, steering wheel, parking brake, all at the same time. The guys in the back seat had their heads turned playing blockers.

"He's left, right, left. Regan, don't let him in, go, go, go. Come on, Regan, block the shit out of him. If you let him by, we're going to be really pissed."

"I'm trying, I'm trying," Regan yelled over the tire squeal. "Damn this track is narrow."

"He's going high, Regan, high, block him, block him," came the screams from the back seat.

"High, there's nothing there but grass," Regan yelled back.

"Exactly, that's where he is, on the grass. Look, here comes the guardrail. Regan, squeeze him up to the guardrail, he'll have to bail."

No sooner was that said than Lenny grabbed the steering wheel and yanked it down to the right. Rick had been in that position before and he also knew who else was in our car. So he knew to expect the unexpected. As I turned and looked over my shoulder to see what his next move would be, the only thing I could see was his grill. It was inches from our rear bumper and it swung hard to the left.

"Inside, inside, he's going inside," I yelled as Regan, or Lenny, I'm not quite sure who, pulled hard to the left. The poor front tires on our car were screaming for all they were worth, which by the way is not much. The car went into an nauseating state of under steer. Regan had the steering wheel cranked to full lock, and the throttle at wide open. Now this was about to get really interesting. The go-kart track was ten feet wide, not thirty feet wide like a racetrack. Just as we were at the apex, *BANG*, Rick hammered us in the left rear quarter panel.

"Oh shit," Regan yelled as the car started to spin with the back end going toward the tire wall.

"You gonna take that shit, Regan? Hit him back," Lenny yelled.

Regan's hands were flailing around the steering wheel like there was no tomorrow. The rear of the car continued to rotate as I looked out my window and saw the tire wall coming up fast. I suddenly realized that there was a large shadow coming over my left shoulder. I turned to see a very large grill, getting larger by the second, heading right at me.

With his front wheels cranked full to the left and his boot hard in the throttle, there was Rick, laughing his ass off. We came to an abrupt halt with an ungodly *THUD*, as tires from the tire wall went flying in every direction. Rick went powering off past us and all we could see was his rear bumper as he reached the finish line.

"Regan."

"I know, I know," Regan replied.

"We're pretty disappointed. You let us down."

"I know, guys, but I swear I'll make it up to you next time."

And Lord knows, there would be a next time.

We pulled off the kart track and back toward the gate to the racetrack, which was now open. We never did find out who opened it. We idled around to the paddock area and placed our battle wagon in park. As we climbed out we heard the sound of a car in pain approaching us. It was Rick and the rest of the winning team. The noise was coming from the left front tire, which had about fifteen degrees of positive camber and six inches of toe out. As Rick came to a halt, half the guys fell out of the car laughing and the other half just got out, shaking their heads.

As we gathered around the cars to inspect the damage, someone looked at Rick's front tire and made this quiet observation: "Yep, it's fucked."

Our car, or rather Regan's car, had tire marks down the right side from bumper to bumper. Fortunately it was mostly cosmetics, at least that's what we tried to tell Regan.

"I sure am glad these things aren't on my credit card," someone said.

No one saw him coming, but we all heard that familiar voice at the same time.

"What's going on?" It was Hank.

"Got any tools?" Rick asked calmly. "We need to do an alignment."

We all broke out into a fit of laughter.

Hank looked at the car, then at us, then turned and walked away, shaking his head. We were pretty sure he turned away so we couldn't see him grin. At the same time, he was pissed.

We opened the trunk to check for tools. There was nothing but a jack and a tire iron.

"I'll run down to Canadian Tire and pick up some tools," Rick offered.

"Okay, I'll jack this thing up and see what kind of damage you did," I said.

"Me?" he said, grinning.

It only made sense that Rick and I should take care of the repairs, since we were both mechanics. Just as we got the front tire off, we heard a screech of tires being abused. We heard that a lot. It was Rick returning with the tools.

"What did you get?" I asked him.

"An adjustable wrench and a hammer," he said, pulling the cheapest tools you could find out of a bag.

"Perfect. I'm sure they'll work just fine," I said.

I slid under the car, which was being held up with a flimsy bumper jack that can be found in the trunks of most North American cars. I took the adjustable wrench and loosened the bolts holding the spindle to the strut. I also loosened the tie rod end so that I could adjust the toe. As I tried to adjust the strut, I realized it was held way too tight onto the spindle and wouldn't budge. After several minutes of trying to move it, I finally gave up. I slid out from under the car and said to what was now an audience, "I have an idea."

I grabbed the handle of the floor jack and started to jack it to the top. When I got it to the last click, the front bumper was about four feet in the air.

"Okay, stand back," I warned. I put my foot on the front fender of the car and pushed as hard as I could. It didn't really take much force before the front of the car started to creak and lean slowly to the right. The car made this godawful *KEEEHK* sound as it slammed down onto the pavement. Just as planned, the first thing to hit the ground was the front brake rotor, with more than enough force to drive the strut adjustment loose and move it to just about where it needed to be.

I picked up the bent jack and wedged it back under the bumper, which was now on the ground. The poor old car looked like a dog that had just had one of its front legs shot out from underneath it. I jacked the car up just enough to get back under it to tighten the bolts that I had loosened, adjusted the toe, and replaced the wheel. Then I lowered the car back to the ground and stood back about twenty feet. I lifted my thumb up and closed one eye as I lined up the wheel to the fender.

"About half a degree of negative camber and zero toe. Perfect," I said as everyone started howling.

"That worked pretty good," Rick said. "Let's go out on the track and see how it handles with its new alignment."

"Okay, I'm driving," I said as I jumped into the car.

It actually drove pretty good. The steering wheel wasn't exactly straight – in fact it was pretty much upside down. As I drove down pit lane I looked in the mirror and saw the other rental car come charging after me. I couldn't see who was driving.

Stones flying, foot to the floor, we entered the front straight in the lead and I had every intention of keeping it. We finished lap one and were still leading, but the other guys were going hell-bent for leather and had no intention of giving up.

As we veered to the left and set up for the carousel at the end of the front straight we were doing about a hundred miles an hour. Rick, who was sitting beside me, calmly said, "Watch out for that big" – *BANG SCREEEEEECH WAM BANG* – "hole at the apex."

"That one?" I asked.

"Yeah, that one."

— — —

"Hey, Bud, you okay?" Cathy asked.

I had been off to a place that I would visit many times over the next few months. A place that was guaranteed to make me smile. My memory bank. I realized that I hadn't answered my mother's question about what Rick did for a living.

"It's kind of hard to explain," I said. "He's a race-car driver and teaches other people to drive."

13
MY GUARDIAN ANGEL

"Can we use that TV and VCR?" Cathy asked the head nurse, pointing to equipment on a roll cart sitting in the corner.

"Sure," she said. "It's not like anyone else in here is going to use it."

Cathy grabbed my hand. "Let's go."

"Go where?"

"Come on. You'll see."

Once in our car, Cathy directed me without letting me in on our destination. As we came up to a small strip mall, she told me to park in front of Blockbuster Video. She ran inside with a level of enthusiasm I hadn't seen for some time.

"Do you have *Days of Thunder*?" she asked the girl behind the counter, who looked over at a young, clean-shaven teenage boy, who said, "We sure do. It's over this way."

Back at the ICU, Cathy dragged the large cart with the TV and VCR over to Rick's bed. She found an outlet right beside the *click, besheeeh* machine.

As *Days of Thunder* came to life, she cranked up the volume and instructed the nurse to rewind and start the tape over when it came to the end. She explained that the doctors had told us that familiar sounds would be good for Rick. And there was no more familiar a sound to him than that of a race car.

– – –

Cathy never failed to amaze me in her support for my racing addiction. I thought back to when we went to Mosport for the first race of the 1991 season. There had been many high-profile racing series in the late 1980s in Canada, but many of their sponsors had pulled out. Rick had just come off the worst of his three seasons in the Rothmans Porsche Turbo Cup Series. This year he would bring a Porsche 944 S2 to the Canadian Firehawk Championship and I would be spending my race weekends in the cockpit of a formula car.

The Esso Protec Series was the highest-level National Formula car series in Canada. In early 1990 I went to Florida and bought the Formula Ford that won the US National Championship. I left for Florida the day after Christmas, just as Cathy and I were preparing to move into our brand new house. Neither of us had any idea how we were going to make our brand new mortgage payments. And pay for the new race car I had just bought with borrowed money. We had some sponsorship support, but as usual it wasn't enough. For some reason Cathy never once said a word to me about buying that car and making the commitment to go racing. Perhaps she knew it wouldn't do her any good to complain.

I found out later that she was sure we were going to lose the house. But she never said a word. She came racing with me and stood beside me through the entire season. The Esso Protec Series was considered one of the most competitive Professional Formula Ford Series in North America, typically involving forty to forty-five cars, any ten or twelve of which could win on any day.

As we pulled into Mosport in our 1980 Ford Cube van that I had converted into a motorhome, sort of, we drove past a lineup of tractor trailers filled with race cars. It was the weekend of May 24, the weekend that kicks off racing season at Mosport every year. Since I knew this was going to be a very tough year, I had decided to bring up an engineer from Phoenix, Ray Germain as well as a few guys from St. Catharines. Ray was perhaps the single most brilliant race engineer I knew at that time. He had engineered the past two National Championships at Road Atlanta.

As Cathy and I unloaded the car out of the trailer, it was raining and as cold as normal for Mosport – about three degrees above freezing. Ray, who had lived his whole life in Phoenix, was standing there with his hands buried in his arm pits.

"This is the coldest winter day I have ever experienced in my life," he said through chattering teeth.

Cathy and I laughed. "Man, this is spring," I said.

"Well, if this is spring then why do you live here?"

One of the trailers in the paddock belonged to a new young rookie. A rookie everyone had been talking about all winter. He was straight out of go-karts and had won national and international championships. His name was Greg Moore and he had all the makings of a championship effort. He was sixteen or seventeen years old, the same age I was when I started racing. The main difference between us that when I started racing, some fourteen years earlier, I didn't have three full-time mechanics and a race engineer. I had Cathy. It was Cathy and me against the world. Even when others were there to help us – we had a couple of weekend warriors who would help us from time to time – they weren't living the effort like Cathy and I were. They hadn't put their house on the line to be there. I had, and that was my choice. And Cathy had, and that was my choice, too, I guess.

We had one more disadvantage. There were about eight or ten teams running brand new 1991 Van Dieman Race cars from England. Cathy and I were running a 1984 American-built Swift. Now maybe our car was seven or eight years old, but it was a pretty nice old car.

We spent Wednesday and Thursday testing and tweaking the car to make it better. When I was out on the track, Cathy was there in the pits, taking times, mine and everyone else's. She communicated my lap times to me and handed me the time sheets when I came into the pits. We discussed what changes needed to be made to make the car better and then went back to the paddock and began working on it. During the next session we repeated everything, over and over and over again. Never satisfied. Or maybe just never done. If we weren't the quickest, we had work to do. Time, money, darkness didn't matter. We just worked and worked late into the night.

On Friday the crowd trickled in as we prepared to go out for the first official practice session.

After practice Cathy and I discussed the session. We looked over at Greg's trailer and saw five or six people swarming his car. Greg was riding his BMX bike around the paddock. At this point we hadn't talked to Greg yet. Later that year we would become friends, with a huge amount of mutual respect.

We were called to the grid for qualifying. Qualifying is perhaps the most stressful time of a race weekend. When you were in a series as competitive as this one, you needed to start up front to finish up front. Cathy understood my need for quiet, but I knew she didn't fully understand why it was so important to me to win. I have never understood it myself. I guess I was living up to Rick's motto: "Show me a good loser and I'll show you a loser." If there ever was a sore loser in this world – that would be me. I knew Cathy respected, or perhaps accepted, the fact that at this moment nothing was more important to me than qualifying up front. Whatever it took, I was willing to deliver. I shut out the world, including Cathy, yet her support never wavered.

As I pulled into the pit lane from the false grid, I spotted her standing with a couple of our weekend warriors and pulled up beside them. I was waiting for the entire field to go by in order to get a clean spot on the track with no traffic. As I finished my standard count to thirty, I didn't dare look at her. Cathy never really said she was nervous during these times, but she didn't have to. Her face said it all. I just closed the visor of my helmet and headed toward pit exit. At the end of the qualifying session, the time sheet told it all: Stephen Adams, Greg Moore, Chris Bye. And then the rest of the field.

Not bad for a couple working out of a cube van competing against all those big rigs. Especially considering that the cube van not only was our work truck, it was also our hotel room.

Not that we advertised the fact that we were sleeping in a cube van all weekend. It didn't matter to us that all of the other teams finished their days and headed off to a restaurant and a nice clean cozy hotel. Well it mattered, but we didn't let it get to us. Most women would have been bitching and moaning about sleeping in a truck. Not Cathy.

Sunday morning the racetrack was packed with fans. I stayed pretty much to myself, not really wanting anyone around. As I sat in the car on the pre grid I looked over at Cathy. She was trying her best to hide her nervousness. Greg was there in his car, surrounded by mechanics and his race engineer Steve Challis. Stephen Adams was in his car, and his mechanics, Ken Robbins and Chris Wibley, were tending to last-minute adjustments. The announcer was preparing the fans for what he described as a "barn burner." He went through the qualifying times and pointed out just how close the top fifteen cars were.

He also prepared everyone for what, in my opinion, is one of the most exciting moments of any motorsport: the standing start. During a standing start, all forty or forty-five cars are lined up side by side with just a few feet between them. At the front of the grid are a series of five red lights. All five lights come on together and then within a few seconds they begin to go out, one by one. At this point every driver brings their engine rpm up to somewhere around 7000. The second the last light goes out, everyone side steps the clutch and tires begin to smoke as the gaggle of cars begin to head into turn 1 – many of them with interlocked wheels. A real recipe for disaster. One wrong move and *SLAM*, you're into the guardrail. And if you qualified at the front, a few dozen cars now have to miss you as you sit sideways across the track. Just another one of a thousand reasons I love this sport so much.

"Two minutes. Start your engines."

Cathy reached into the car and gave my hand a squeeze. "Have fun, I love you."

After the craziness of the standing start, I spent the next forty-five minutes doing everything in my power to stay with and try to get by Greg, who was being led by Adams. We finished in that order. Adams, Moore, and Bye stood on the three steps of the podium. I looked at Cathy as the three of us covered each other and everyone in Victory Lane with champagne. She saw the frustration in my eyes over finishing third, but the joy that was there, too, for being on the podium.

At the end of the season we finished second in the championship behind Stephen Adams. Greg had done a great job, but a few rookie mistakes cost him a higher position. Walking up on stage at the banquet to accept my – no, make that our – second-place trophy was one of the sweetest moments in my – no, make that our – career.

14
FEAR OF THE UNKNOWN

A few days after Rick's surgery, we finally got a chance to meet Connie, Rick's girlfriend, or I should say *one* of Rick's girlfriends. After Connie called, Wendy had also called and said she was coming down to Winston-Salem. So there we all were, Mom, Dad, Cathy, Connie, Wendy, and I, all standing at Rick's bedside.

Connie and Wendy hit it off immediately. It would be difficult not to get along with Wendy, a lovable and pleasant person.

As we all walked out into the hall, Cathy said the only reason she was staying strong was that, besides Mom, she was one of the only women in the hospital who hadn't slept with Rick. We laughed.

I watched Wendy and Connie spend time together, standing on either side of Rick's bed, each holding a hand. Each looking at him. Each talking to him. Each praying that he would answer them. Each not caring which one he would look at first. Each not caring which one he would talk to first.

They even went out and had a few drinks together. I have no idea what they talked about, but they obviously had one thing in common: a deep love for Rick. Wendy's was the love you have for a friend – a friend you would go to the ends of the earth for. A friend who could do no wrong, no matter what. Connie's love was of a more intimate kind. There were no real signs of this love in the way she talked to him or touched him, but you could tell.

By the end of the weekend it had been exactly eleven days since Rick's accident and seven days since his surgery. It was looking like Cathy and I had to think about getting home. We decided there was nothing more we could do at the hospital at this point. I wasn't so sure anyone could do anything to help. We had personal things to attend to like bills and a mortgage. I wondered how hard it would be to leave. Would Rick wake up after we left?

We decided we would leave the next day, exactly one week after the operation. Rick still hadn't come to. It was hard to believe it had only been a week and a half since we last saw Hailey. During the trip home, neither of us had much to say. Twelve hours of silence.

As I walked into the house I heard the phone ringing. I grabbed the phone in our bedroom.

"Mr. Bye, this is John and I'm calling regarding your cell-phone bill."

I don't know how many times I had explained this to these people, but here it went one more time. "I reported the phone stolen last fall," I said. "It was stolen when I was in Utah. They told me I had to get a police report number, so I called the police and got that number. I was told the phone would be deactivated as of that date. The following month a bill showed up at my office and it had a $250 cancellation fee and another $200 worth of calls that were made after I reported it stolen. I was told that it was no problem and that whoever I was talking to would take care of it. But a month later another bill showed up and I went through the same thing all over again. This has now been going on now for several months and to be honest it's getting old."

"Well, Mr. Bye, you see I don't really care. This matter has been turned in for collection and you will pay it."

"Oh, really ..."

This guy proceeded to tell me how I was going to go to a bank or Western Union the next day to wire the amount owed.

"What did you say your name was again?" I asked.

"John, Chris. My name is John."

"Well, John, listen carefully and if you can't hear me, read my lips." I gave him some very specific and unprintable advice. "Did you get that, John?" I asked and then proceeded to bang the phone on top of the dresser.

Just then Cathy walked in. "Stressed a little?" she asked.

An hour later the phone rang again. It was Mom.

"How is he?" I asked.

"He's waking up, " she said with great excitement in her voice. "Not long after you guys left they came in and gave him a blood transfusion. It was like a miracle. As the new blood went in he started to open his eyes. By the time the blood bag emptied, his eyes were wide open. It's really a miracle."

"That's great. Is he talking? Does he know where he is or what happened to him? Does he know you?" I asked in one long breath.

"No, he's just lying there looking up at the ceiling, but I know it won't be long. He's doing great. Oh, they said they're going to move him."

"Move him where?"

"Toronto – they said they're taking him to Toronto."

"Toronto? What do you mean? Who said they are taking him to Toronto?"

"The nurses."

"Don't worry, he's not going anywhere. Did you ever sign any of those papers that the insurance company sent?"

"No," she said, "and I won't."

As it turned out, Rick did have insurance. He had bought a travel policy that covered medical insurance whenever he was out of the country. When we first found the insurance card in his wallet I called the 1-800 number on the back of it and explained who I was and the situation. The person I spoke to was very understanding and helpful. They assured me that everything would be taken care of and that we shouldn't worry about anything.

Well, that was actually where their support ended. In the past few weeks, their attitude had gone from great to outright despicable.

The company began a harassment campaign by fax. They were vague in their conversations and you could never get the same person twice. When you called back and asked for "Michelle," you would get, "Sir, do you have a last name? There are hundreds of people working in this office and without a last name there is no way I could find anyone."

It took awhile but it became apparent to me that the whole thing was a setup to avoid paying out claims. But things with them weren't over. They hadn't even started.

"I'll make some calls and will call you back as soon as I know anything," I told Mom. "I'm sure they can't transport him without our consent, so don't worry. He isn't going anywhere right now."

I got Dr. Chang on the line and asked, "What's this I hear about Rick being transported home?"

"I got a call yesterday from the insurance company," he began, "and they asked me if Rick was stable enough to be transported to Toronto. I said he would probably survive a medivac jet ride up there but that I wouldn't recommend a road trip. I asked them why they were asking and they said his policy states that as soon as the patient is stable enough to be transported to their home province or territory, they are."

"Well, as soon as Rick is back in Ontario our government health insurance will take over and the insurance company will be off the hook," I said. "That's why they want him moved. Do you know if they are talking about taking him to a level one trauma center?"

"No, we didn't really get that far."

"Mike, I don't want him moved. I know he's not good, but everyone in the family feels he couldn't be in better hands. You can't let him leave. I don't know if you're aware of the health-care situation up here in Canada, but it's not good. And it doesn't have anything to do with the quality of our doctors or nurses, it's just getting to them. There's a possibility he would get the care he needs up here. But there's also a possibility that he won't. And that's an unknown we just don't need to deal with right now. He needs to stay there with you and your team."

"Chris, don't worry. He isn't going anywhere. They can't take him anywhere without my approval. I don't answer the phones around here and I'm not going to return their calls."

I figured now was as good a time as any to make another call to the insurance company. I was given to someone named David who said he was taking care of Rick's case.

"I have just returned from North Carolina and I got a call that you guys were thinking of moving Rick to Toronto," I said.

"Mr. Bye, how is your brother?"

"Well, he's in a coma and has been for about two weeks now."

I couldn't put my finger on it but something about him annoyed me. Maybe it was the tone of his voice. He talked like someone who has something over on you. There was this arrogance about him that made me want to say something I knew I shouldn't.

"Well, Chris – may I call you Chris?"

"Yeah, no problem, Dave," I replied with my guard up.

"We have sent several documents to Rick that we need to have signed and there has been little or no cooperation from either Rick or your family. Look, we would like to see this matter straightened up as much as you would. But you and your family have not been cooperative up to this point."

"Let me ask you something, David. What address did you send these documents to?"

"To 2500 Wycroft Road, Oakville, Ontario, Unit 24."

"Well, you see, David, that might be the problem. That is Rick's shop address. Rick isn't there to collect his mail. He's lying in a coma in North Carolina. And our entire family is down there with him. There's no one there to get his mail."

"You see, Chris, this is what I am talking about," David said in a smartass tone that had come to the surface. "I know what your family is like. If you keep up this attitude, I will just go ahead and cancel the entire claim."

"What did you say?"

"Pardon?"

"What did you say about my family?"

"I said that your family has an attitude and has been uncooperative."

"Really, David, an attitude. Let me ask you something, David. Have you ever walked into an intensive care unit and seen a friend or family member lying in a bed with tubes going in and out of everywhere? A big plastic bolt screwed into their head? A breathing tube jammed down their throat and a feeding tube stuck up their nose? A respirator clicking away in the corner breathing for them, keeping them alive? Legs hanging in traction with bones obviously not pointed in the right direction? Their skin looking like it's about to burst because it's stretched so tight? All this after being told that there is was a two percent chance of them coming out of the ER? Tell me, David, have you ever had that privilege?"

"No, Chris, I haven't," he replied, still defiant.

"Well, David, I hope you never have to, but if one day you do, I hope you don't have insurance with your company. Now as far as you canceling the policy, somehow I don't think I'm talking to the president of the company at 10 o'clock on Sunday night." My heart rate was up to at least two hundred. Cathy was just standing there looking at me, shaking her head.

I was on a roll. I decided to call a doctor I knew who was also a Porsche Club member. I explained the latest to him and he said I should find out where they were thinking of taking him and to make sure they had a level one trauma center. He reminded me that this fight was probably not over – that in fact it had just begun. He also mentioned that I should ask how he would be admitted, through normal channels or through the ER.

I called the hospital in Toronto and found out that they did have a level one trauma center and that Rick would be admitted through the ER. I asked the person on the phone if they could guarantee us in writing that he would not lie in a hallway somewhere until there was a bed ready, and they said they couldn't make that guarantee. At that moment, our minds were made up. Rick was not going to be moved.

After being home for a couple days it quickly became apparent that I was not the only one with bills to pay. Rick had a few of his own. I received a call from Rick's landlord, Angelo, letting me know that the rent at the shop was due, to the tune of $2,400.

Angelo and the others Rick owed money to understood the difficulty he was in, but that didn't mean they weren't anxious to be paid.

We had no idea how long Rick's recovery was going to last, but we could see we were going to need financial help to get through this. Also, we had no idea who else might call looking for money from Rick. I decided it was time to make another difficult call, to Ed Werner, longtime friend and one of the founding partners of Trivial Pursuit.

"Chris, just name it," Ed said when I told him of our predicament.

"I guess maybe ten thousand will help, but like I said, I don't have any idea how long this thing is going to go on."

"I will have Linda make out a check. You can pick it up this afternoon."

"Ed, I hate to have to ask."

"Chris," Ed said cutting me off. "Don't worry about it. I know you wouldn't ask if you didn't have to."

I vowed to myself that Ed would be the first person to get paid back as soon as this thing was over, whenever that might be.

15

"I'M ASCARED"

The next day we were pleased to learn that the insurance company that held Rick's automotive policy, Wawanessa, would pay for flights for the family. Cathy and I decided that I would go back to North Carolina on Wednesday, February 8, with Hailey. Cathy had to travel to Toronto to attend an annual Shoppers Drug Mart conference for store associates and managers.

Hailey and I flew out of Buffalo airport en route to Greensboro airport, about twenty miles from Winston-Salem. We arrived late in the afternoon and checked in at the Hawthorne. I called the hospital and found out Rick had been moved from the ICU to the eleventh floor. Mom had been telling us that Rick was doing great and really coming along, and I was looking forward to seeing him looking better.

"Daddy, I don't want to go to the hospital," Hailey said.

"Why, Hailey?"

"I'm ascared."

I told her it was okay, but she didn't seem convinced. I gave her the option of coming to the hospital or staying in the hotel room alone. Of course she agreed to come with me. And of course I wasn't about to leave her at the hotel. But she wasn't so sure of that.

Hailey was very apprehensive as we pulled into the hospital

parkade. As we walked toward the hospital, hand in hand, the enormity of her uncle's situation hit her.

"This building is gynormous," she said looking up, almost falling backwards. Once we were in the lobby, she looked around and realized that maybe this wasn't such a bad place. She was doing fine until we reached the elevator. I almost had to drag her into it. As we headed up the elevator to Rick's new floor, she backed into the corner.

"I'm not going in Uncle Rick's room," she said.

"Don't you want to see Uncle Rick?"

"No. Well, yes, but I'm ascared."

"What are you afraid of?"

"I don't know. I just am."

"Okay, tell you what. You wait out in the hall while I go in. I will see how he's doing and I will come out and get you if he's up to seeing you. Is that okay?"

She nodded sheepishly as the elevator boinged and the doors slid open. As we walked down the hall, her eyes darted left, right, up, down. She watched intently as people walked by. Then she climbed into a chair outside Rick's room and pulled her knees up to her chin, wrapping her arms around them as if she was freezing.

As I stood there beside her something didn't feel right to me. I had gotten used to ICU 5B – its sounds, smells, sights, the nurses, the doctors. I wasn't sure what experiences the eleventh floor would hold for me.

Mom was sitting in a chair in the corner of Rick's room. Dad was out getting coffee.

"He's doing great," Mom said.

Time for an eye appointment, Mom, I thought. Rick looked ten times worse than just a few days ago. He looked dead. His eyes were sunken and hollow. He couldn't have weighed more than ninety pounds. Mercifully, his breathing was slow and steady and he was no longer hooked up to the *click, besheeeh* machine.

"He has been squeezing my hand. And the nurses keep telling us how well he's doing," Mom said.

This is good? I thought. He no longer had a feeding tube and was being fed intravenously. I wasn't sure what I expected, but this sure wasn't it. Once again I had let my guard down. I knew I had to stop doing that. It wasn't like me to ever do that, not with my parents, Cathy, or even Hailey. If I did, someone might get inside. I just could not have that.

I stood there listening to the silence, broken occasionally with a nurse call to some room and some *boing boing* sound, which I was sure meant something to someone. I kept wondering whether Rick was sleeping, in a coma, in a partial coma, or perhaps just under the influence of the drugs, whatever they were.

Looking for an excuse to leave the room, I told Mom I needed to go check on Hailey. Out in the hall, I looked left, then right. No Hailey. Where the hell could she have gone?

I was heading for the nurses' station when I heard a rustling sound. Hailey was no longer in the chair in the hall. She was under it, all curled up, vibrating.

"Hey, what are you doing under there?" I said quietly. I bent down and looked into her eyes, which were spouting big tears. "Hey, come here. What's wrong?"

"I'm ascared, Daddy. I want to go home," she said as she slid out from under the chair and stretched her arms out for me to lift her to safety. She wrapped her arms around my neck so tight she was choking me. Her whole body was shaking. She sobbed like a baby, trying to catch her breath as she buried her head between my shoulder and neck.

"It's okay, kid. Nothing here is going to hurt you."

"I know. I just don't like it here. I want to go home."

"We can't go home for a few days. How about we go back to the hotel and go swimming? Would that be okay?" I felt her head nod in the affirmative.

I motioned Mom to come out. She spent a few minutes with Hailey, helping me settle her down. While we were out there a couple of nurses went into the room and wheeled Rick out. Hailey scrunched back into the chair, which she was sitting on again. She put her hands to her mouth and pushed back into the chair as far as she could. Her eyes locked on Rick as they slowly pushed him past us and down the hall. His eyes were staring straight up, gliding like a seagull soaring, not focusing on anything.

"Where are they taking him?" Hailey asked quietly.

"For another test," I replied. She ignored me, her eyes fixed on the now empty hall.

"Mom, I'm going to take Hailey back to the hotel so we can go swimming," I said. "Give us a call when you and Dad get back there and maybe we'll go for something to eat."

"Okay, drive careful," she said.

It never really occurred to me before, but Mom had said "drive careful" every time any of us parted company since we got to North Carolina.

It was very difficult having Hailey with me. She would not go into Rick's room. It was tough trying to balance her between Mom and me. She spent her days in Winston-Salem quiet, and, for the most part, confused. She asked every day when Uncle Rick was going to wake up. My reply was always the same: "I wish I knew, sweetheart. I wish I knew."

I called Cathy and we decided I would bring Hailey home and Cathy would return with me.

16

THERE BUT NOT THERE

The word was out that Rick was out of the ICU. People were asking about seeing him. We called everyone we could think of who might stop by, letting them know we were suspending visitation till further notice – that this was in everyone's best interest, especially Rick's.

It would have been upsetting for visitors to see Rick. He opened his eyes now fairly regularly and moved around, but he was by no means awake. He wasn't aware of anything around him. Now that he was out of the ICU, the level of care went down. Not that the care wasn't still exemplary, but the eleventh floor didn't have the nurse-to-patient ratio of the ICU.

Waking from a coma isn't what I thought it would be. When we first walked into the room and saw that his eyes were open, we thought, "Oh my god, he's awake!" But we quickly realized that his eyes may have been open, but there was nobody home. He wasn't seeing anything. You could pass your hands over his face – no reaction.

This seemed to go on forever. Then, around February 13, we walked into the room and he was looking at us. Again our hearts pounded with excitement followed by the realization that while his eyes happened to be pointed in our direction, they weren't really looking at anything.

The next stage – when his eyes followed you around the room – was a big one. That happened the week of February 16. There was no thought, no expression, no emotion, just movement, but to me this was a real milestone. It meant that the lights were on *and* someone was home.

Rick was now more dependent on us – in particular, on Mom. When we were in the ICU, he had tubes in place to take care of his bodily functions. Now, since he was pretty much still comatose, he was like an infant. He needed the type of care my mother had given to him when he was a baby. But Mom was no longer the young, energetic mother of an infant. And she and Dad looked about twenty years older than when we first arrived in North Carolina, just over two weeks ago.

Watching Rick was becoming more difficult for me by the day. Something was bothering me and I couldn't quite figure out what it was. I would go back to the hotel completely spent. I found that the more time I spent at the hospital, the more time I spent sliding. I knew Rick was getting better. So why was I getting worse?

Rick's there-but-not-there phase seemed to be lasting for weeks, but in reality it had only been a couple of days since Cathy and I had been back in North Carolina. It was becoming more and more difficult for me to be in the room with him. He had yet to speak a word. Sometimes he looked like he wanted to say something, and at others he just stared off into some distant world. I just didn't know what to say, think, or do.

At times when his eyes were open, the nurses tried to prop him up in bed. But he was like a rag doll. He had no muscle control. He had no control of any kind. He just lay there, propped up, looking pathetic. I felt ashamed for thinking that.

I would sit beside his bed and pass my hand over his eyes every once in a while – nothing, no blink, no reaction, just that stare.

The nurses quickly came to hate me. Well, maybe hate is too strong a word, but they sure didn't like me very much. My parents are good people who don't like making waves, so they were very patient when it came to Rick's needs. I am not patient at all. If Rick needed his bed changed I simply walked up to the nurses' station and said, "Rick needs his bed changed." The reply was always the same: "Okay, Mr. Bye, we will get to that just as soon as possible."

"Fine. When will that be?"

"Well, all of the nurses are busy at this time and just as soon as we get a minute we will be there."

"Okay," I would reply, standing in the same spot.

"Mr. Bye, there really is no need."

"Hey, you look like you have a minute," I would say to the first nurse I saw. "Can you come and change Rick's bed?"

The nurse I was speaking to would get this confused look on her face and look at whoever was behind the desk, who would nod to her to go ahead. I knew it was just to get me out of her hair. The way I figured, I wasn't there to win any popularity contest. Rick could not fend for himself, so I would fend for him.

I knew that if the tables were turned, Rick would be there for me and would be as miserable and ornery as necessary to get me what I needed.

Rick had been spending a lot more time awake in the last couple of days. Well, you really couldn't call it awake, but his eyes were open and he seemed to be moving them a lot more. At times he seemed to be able to ask for things. I don't really know how he asked, because he didn't talk or point or gesture.

He was just starting to move his hands and feet, but with very little control. He looked at us when we asked him something. It was a small step, but at least it was a step. He was now spending time looking at the TV and out the window, especially the window. Whether the drapes were open or closed made no difference. He just stared. He was also starting to recognize when someone entered the room. It was nothing other than a look. He would turn his head either to the television or the window. He was in his own world, but at least he was in some world.

Into this twilight zone came an unexpected visitor.

"Hi, I'm Rick's physical therapist," said an attractive blond girl. She said what her name was but I was so caught off guard that I didn't get it.

"Hi," I replied, looking at my mother. She looked as confused as

I did. What the hell does this therapist think she's going to accomplish, we were both thinking. Rick doesn't even know what planet he's on and you want to start therapy.

"Here, let's prop his bed up," she said. She grabbed the bed control and pressed the button. As the head of the bed started to rise, Rick started sliding to the left. She pulled Rick up into a sitting position. Sort of. She was going about her work as if this was just another normal day. I guess it was for her.

"Rick, do you know what this is?" she asked, taking a toothbrush out of her pocket and putting it in front of his face.

Rick looked around and then focused, sort of, on the toothbrush. This was the first time I had actually seen him focus on anything. He just kept looking and then slowly nodded his head. Mom and I stared in amazement. Rick slowly moved his gaze from the therapist to the toothbrush, from the toothbrush back to the therapist, and then back to us. And then to the closed curtains of the window. He looked back her way and slowly nodded his head again. Up then down. Not the way a normal person nodded. His head fell and he caught it, only to have it fall again.

My mother had been telling me that he was acknowledging things. I just thought she was imagining things and I and didn't want to disappoint her. But now I was seeing it myself.

The therapist placed the toothbrush in Rick's hand and wrapped his bony fingers around it. "Rick, what do you do with it?" she asked.

Come on, show her, I was yelling inside. I looked over at Mom and knew she was thinking the same thing.

Rick's gaze moved from the toothbrush to the therapist, to Mom, and then to me. His look was blank. And then it was as if he had a light-bulb moment. He didn't smile, but his eyebrows raised a little, slowly. At least they seemed to. He very slowly started to raise the toothbrush. Up, up, up the toothbrush went.

He knows, he's back, I can't believe it, this is amazing, I thought as the toothbrush neared his mouth.

Rick moved the head of the toothbrush toward his mouth and then continued straight up landing it somewhere between his forehead and his right ear. He then lamely started to brush his hair with it. Forward, then back. Forward, then back.

Rick looked to the therapist, as if for affirmation. It was a good thing he didn't look at me. My mouth was hanging open.

"Good, Rick, good," the therapist said.

He thinks a toothbrush is a hairbrush and this is good? I thought. What am I missing? Why am I not celebrating like everyone else in the room? Maybe he'd be better off ... maybe we'd all be better off?

My mother looked at me as if she knew what I was thinking. I had to leave the room, but I was afraid to stand. I didn't know if my legs would support me. My knees felt like rubber.

I somehow found the strength to stand and backed out of the room before Rick could look at me. Out in the hall I collapsed into the chair that Hailey had hid under earlier. Hell, hiding under the chair didn't seem like such a bad idea at that moment. I kept trying to stand up, but my legs were not receiving the signal from my brain.

I waited till the therapist left and finally was able to get up and head back into the room. Rick was sleeping and Mom had her head back into a magazine as if nothing had happened. Maybe nothing had happened. I guess it was good that he could move his arms and knew that it was some kind of brush. I knew what I was supposed to feel but I just couldn't feel it.

I closed my eyes. My mind drifted off to a place and a time far, far away. A place that, once again, helped me keep my sanity.

— — —

In 1993 the team loaded up the trailer and headed down the road for Sebring, Florida. We were going to compete in the Firestone Firehawk 12 Hours of Sebring. This race was held in the fall, unlike the traditional 12 Hours of Sebring, which was always in the spring. Rick had asked me to co-drive with him and his regular teammate, Ray David.

I flew into Orlando with our crew chief, Ted. We grabbed our rental car and headed an hour and a half south to the site of the oldest running sports car race in America. I was both excited and nervous. I had never driven at Sebring, and Rick's Commercial Motorsport Porsche team had just come off another Canadian Firstone Firehawk Championship. I knew Rick and I had a good chance not just of doing well at this race but actually winning it.

After pulling into Sebring, we went to the office to register and get our credentials. I looked at the entry list – eighty-four cars.

When practice time finally came, I stood in the pit lane as Rick turned the key and the Porsche grunted a few times and then snapped to life. *Blat, blat, blat,* the Porsche went as it sat there and idled. Ted reached for his ears and put pressure on both sides of his headset to close out ambient noise. He stood at the front of the car and looked intently into Rick's eyes through the windscreen. Ted nodded a few times and then walked out to the pit wall as Rick slid the Porsche into gear and slowly let out the clutch. *Blat, blat, blat ... ruh, ruh, ruh,* went the Porsche as it gently left the pit box. Rick and I were never ones to slam the throttle down and spin the tires when leaving pit lane in practice. Or during a race, for that matter. It just puts undue stress on the car and its components.

I walked out to the pit wall in my driver's suit and stood beside Ted. The Porsche came into view, perhaps a quarter of a mile away, and in fourth gear. *Sheeew, sheeew, sheeew,* went the cars as they flew by Ted and me for the first time. All eighty-four of them. Rick was in the middle of the endless stream of color and noise. *Oh yeah, baby!*

Rick did the first half of practice before he radioed Ted and told him to get me ready because he was coming in, in a lap or two.

Ted gave me the familiar Ted nod as I walked across pit lane and reached for my helmet.

The KFC Porsche idled slowly down pit lane toward where I squatted on the pit wall. I could feel my pulse in my nostrils. As the car came to a stop I slid off the pit wall and walked around the front of it. The crew covered it like seagulls on fries in a parking lot. Not chaotically, but fast, everyone knowing who was in charge and in which order things were to be done.

I opened the driver's door as Rick hit the release on his six-point safety harness. All six belts sprang in every direction as they gave way to the rubber straps they were attached to. The straps are designed to keep the belts out of the way during driver changes. I reached in and unplugged Rick' s radio plug, which went from his helmet to a plug attached to the roll cage. Rick grabbed the roof of the car with his left hand as his right hand found the side of the seat. In one fluent swoosh, he pulled his knees to his chest and landed both feet on the ground at the same time. I repeated the move, in reverse, and soon found myself where I wanted to be more than anywhere else on earth: strapped into a race car in pit lane and preparing to go to battle with eighty-three other warriors.

"The track is dirty in a few corners from guys going off," Rick yelled over the noise of our idling car and the others sailing by down the pit at a hundred plus miles per hour. "Remember, it's just practice. Don't get sucked into racing anyone out there. It's really crazy, there are cars everywhere, so be careful." Then he plugged in my radio.

I gave one last tug on the belts after they were all hooked up. The car dropped from the jacks as the crew finished checking every-thing and Jeff stepped aside, waving me clear. *Runt, runt, runt,* the Porsche went, chugging to life as I slowly let out the clutch and headed down the very long pit lane.

The light at the exit of pit lane was green, giving me the all clear to hammer the throttle to the floor and hang on as I entered corner 1, leaving pit lane.

First, second, third gear ... I gunned down on corner 2. Brake, downshift, turn in, still going fairly slowly as I waited for the tires to heat up. The Porsche hit the apex and then slowly started to leave the left edge of the road. I turned in tighter but was carrying too much speed to hold the car left. As I approached the right side of the road I realized I had just done something stupid. I was carrying too much speed for this decreasing radius corner and I was about to go off the road on the very first lap of a racetrack I had never seen before. Luckily there was nothing to hit as the Porsche slid off the track and onto the grass and gravel. All four wheels were off the road as a train of other cars went flying by my left side. I gathered my composure and headed back onto the track, thinking, "Now that was pretty stupid, moron!"

The weekend went well and our two Commercial Motorsport Porsches qualified in the top ten. Not bad, considering there were factory teams there from just about every manufacturer you could think of. It was decided that Rick would start the race and I would get in at the first pit stop.

On race day, at the drop of the green flag, Rick quickly climbed to second behind David Murry, who was also driving a Porsche.

The race settled into a quick, steady pace. Ted gave me his famous nod and I calmly walked over and picked up my helmet and began preparing myself to get into the car.

As I crouched on the pit wall and Rick brought the Porsche down pit lane one hour and thirty minutes after he left, I could almost taste the tension. Ted reminded Rick on the radio of the pit lane speed limit.

The crew came to life as the Porsche hit its marks in the pit box. The brakes squealed loudly as they always do when they're hot. And hot they were. Smoke rolled out of the front wheel wells as the crew lifted the car and prepared to bolt on four new Firestone Firehawk racing tires. While they did that they also checked the brake pads, topped up the engine oil, checked the CV joints, cleaned the radiator, cleaned all windows, strapped in a new pilot, me, filled the drink bottle, and dropped the car off the jacks. All in about a minute and a half. Now that's service.

"Sixty miles per hour is the pit lane speed limit ... *sixty*," Ted mumbled into the radio. "Do not get a Stop and Go for speeding in the pits."

"Nooo problem," I replied. The pit lane light was green and the throttle was on the floor. *Let's go, baby!*

The Porsche was well warmed up and the crew had kept us in the top five with their usual outstanding pit work.

First ... second ... third ... brake ... second ... I slammed the throttle back down as I straightened the steering wheel and worked my way back up through the gearbox. Fourth gear was what you needed as you entered the very long back straight at Sebring. The tach bounced off the rev limiter and you quickly grabbed fifth. By the end of the back straight I would see 7000 rpm in fifth gear. Now that was flying, somewhere around 160 or 170 miles per hour.

There is perhaps only one thing a Porsche does better than go fast ... and that is stop fast. Porsche brakes are hard to beat. Especially at that speed. As I approached the braking areas, the guys in the Firebirds and Camaros were about to quickly disappear in my mirrors. American Iron has the torque and horsepower to keep up with the Porsches, but they're not even in the ballpark when it comes to brakes.

Racetracks use braking markers as you enter corners. These

markers are normally numbered 4, 3, 2, 1. They are there only as reference points. The North American cars would be hard on the brakes at about the 4 marker. The Porsche would have the throttle mashed to the floor until about halfway between the 3 and 2 marker, leaving the others in its dust ... brake dust, that is.

I settled into a quick comfortable pace, knowing how important it was not to have any contact with any other race cars on the track. Contact would take us out of contention. My ninety-minute stint went by without any trauma. I kept the car comfortably in the top five.

"Pit next lap," Ted mumbled into the headset.

"See you in one," I said, then, for the sake of the pit crew, "Entering the back straight," and then, "Entering pit lane." I made sure the Porsche was right at the pit speed limit, and not one mph slower.

"Sixty is pit lane speed," Ted reminded me.

"Sixty," I replied.

The brakes screeched as I nosed the Porsche in the pit box. Ray was already halfway in the car as I catapulted out and stepped aside.

"Everything's great. The car's awesome," I screamed into his helmet. Ray's eyes were locked straight ahead and he gave me a slight nod. I stepped back, attached the window net, and closed the door. I walked around the back of the car and slid over the pit wall and into the pits and out the back. I reached for my helmet strap ... which was hard to find. I realized that my fingers were trembling. I was having a hard time grabbing the tap attached to the strap.

It's strange how this happens only when you get out of the race car. At least that's how it always is with me. My fingers start to tremble and my breathing becomes rapid. It isn't as if I am nervous. I guess it's the adrenaline catching up with me. I finally calmed my fingers down and got my helmet off, along with my balaclava. Someone walked over and handed me a Gatorade.

"Good job," Jeff said, patting me on the back.

"It ain't over," I said. He grinned and nodded. We were only three hours into a twelve-hour race. And at 170 mph, anything could happen.

My next stint, some three hours later, was fairly routine. We were still solidly in the top five and comfortable.

As I got into the car for my third stint, it was dark. "Be careful," Rick yelled into my helmet as he finished doing up my safety harness. "It is totally black out there. You can't see a thing."

I have always loved racing at night, perhaps because I've done a lot of it, mostly at my home track, Mosport. Rick and I have done so many laps there that we could do them with our eyes closed. And at night it's just like driving with your eyes closed. Your headlights shine into the trees, light up the stars, and blind the drunk race fans lining the circuit. They go just about everywhere but where you want them to.

At Mosport I drive at night by timing. One, two, three, turn. One two three, four, turn. Sebring at night was a very different story. Particularly tonight.

I had run a few laps in night practice on this track but not really enough to get a feel for where everything was. As I rounded the first few corners I realized there were very few – make that *no* – visual markers. There were no trees, no lights, no nothing to give you a reference on this very flat, very fast, airport-based racetrack.

I exited the corner leading onto the very long and fast back straight. I looked into the mirrors at the amazing gaggle of headlights. They were mesmerizing. I looked up out the windshield and into a night completely dark except for the red taillights in front of me.

I reached for fifth gear as the engine stumbled on the rev limiter. Throttle up, clutch down, shifter up and right in one fluid motion, clutch up and throttle slammed back to the floor. Something was wrong. The taillights in front of me were way to my right. A stream of cars out the right side window. Well, I'll be damned, how did all those cars get so far off the racetrack? I continued looking in amazement out the right side of the car. Hell, they must be seventy-five or a hundred feet off the track. I checked the mirror as the car slowly started to rotate to the right. No gaggle of lights. Just total darkness. Oh, oh … It's not them, you moron, it's you.

On leaving the last corner and checking the mirror I had somehow found myself and the Porsche about a hundred feet off the racetrack and out in the middle of some half grass-covered closed runway. The Porsche slowly continued to rotate to the right as I gingerly lifted off the throttle. Don't do anything drastic or all hell will break loose, I thought.

I slowly got the car under control and back to the back straight. Brake, downshift for the corner leading off the back straight and onto the front straight. Throttle jammed and shifter flying.

"Everything okay?" Ted asked as I passed his position in pit lane.

"Just fine," I said. "Just fine."

I brought the Porsche in one more time and Ray jumped back in. I was to have one more stint before the end of the race. A stint that will be etched in my memory forever.

We were still strongly in the top five ten hours in as Rick strapped me in the Porsche once again. He was even more serious now and no one was talking.

The first forty-five minutes went flawlessly. Everything was fine. Then the rain came. Slowly at first, and then a little harder, especially in some areas of the track. That was normal on a road course, especially one four and half miles long.

"You want wets?" Ted's voice echoed in my helmet, referring to rain tires.

"No, I'm good. This thing is great."

"You are pulling away from the guys behind you. You sure you're okay?"

"It's all good," I said as I thought about putting time between me and whoever was behind me.

The Porsche braking in the dry is amazing, but in the wet it is unbelievable. I was out-braking guys off the end of the back straight by a mile. Or at least it felt like a mile. Rick and I have always been comfortable in the rain and I was low in my seat, focused and flying through the rooster tails of water coming off all the other cars, all eighty-three of them. The brake lights in front of me were big and blurry through the flying mist. Several laps went by and I was picking off cars in every corner. One, two, three disappeared as I went by them. Coming off the back straight, the Porsche was like a well-behaved thoroughbred. It did everything I asked of it, including for it to still do 7000 rpm in fifth gear by the end of the straight. Yes sir, no problem. However, this well-mannered thoroughbred was about to become one pissed off bronco. And the ride was not going to be fun.

As my confidence grew I was leaving my braking later and later. This lap I had one ounce too much confidence and left it too late.

How much too late? It didn't much matter. As I jumped on the brake pedal at around 160 mph it felt like I had just pressed my right foot against an oak tree. Nothing. No pedal movement, no depletion of speed, just quiet, dark, rain, 160 mph, and no brakes. A calmness came over me. I took a slow breath.

At the end of the back straight the track does a 180-degree turn and then heads back up the front straight. This is not a problem. The problem is the concrete bridge the track goes under.

The car slowly began to rotate to the right. I slowly turned the steering wheel to the left. The car then slowly began to rotate to the left, and I turned the wheel to the right. The brake pedal was still oak tree stationary. I glanced down quickly at the dash. There to the right was large toggle switch with the letters ABS clearly marked below it. The switch was turned up toward on. I thought about trying to flip the switch down to off. Would that help?

The car snapped so hard to the right it ripped the steering wheel out of my hands. It then began a series of spins, like a nickel flicked by a ten year old. The car was spinning so fast I had no idea where I was or where I was going. I tried, in vain, to reach the ABS switch. The ABS would not let the tires lock up and the car was spinning, but it was also moving all over the racetrack. There is an unwritten rule in racing that if you're headed toward a spinning car, aim for it. The theory is that it won't be there by the time you get there. If the wheels of a spinning car are locked, the car will spin on its axles. The Commercial Motorsport Porsche was spinning with the ABS on, so it, and I, were moving all over the racetrack. And the other twenty or thirty drivers were all heading for me at 160 mph cursing me for not having my foot on the brakes. They could not have been more wrong.

The only thing worse than spinning at 160 mph is not spinning at 160 mph, backwards.

The Porsche suddenly got very quiet and calm. The spinning stopped. I was probably still going well over a hundred miles per hour. Straight, quiet ... and backwards. Toward the concrete bridge. How far? Don't know.

If I put it in first I would probably break something, I thought. I looked down at the shifter. The clutch was in and the engine was idling. I reached for the shifter and pulled it out of fifth. I pulled it left toward me and down as it slid into the second gear gate. I rolled my right foot, which was still hard on the brake pedal, over to the right and caught the edge of the throttle. I squeezed the throttle all the way to the floor. The Porsche engine came to life. *WAAAAANN*, it screamed, at about 6000 rpm. My left foot side stepped the clutch. *WAM*. All hell broke loose. I had no idea what was going on outside the car but I knew the back tires were spinning forward. I kept the gas pedal firmly planted on the floor. An elephant could not have pulled my right foot from the floor.

The car began this loud, noisy, sickening shake that came from deep within. The entire car was vibrating and shaking and screaming in pain. The shifter was bouncing so hard it seemed to hit the roof. I was coming out of my seat as the rear wheels hopped, smoked, and screamed for mercy. The windshield was surely going to come out. My head slammed against the back of the Recaro racing seat, blurring my vision.

It stopped. The Porsche stopped. I eased up on the gas. It was running. Quiet. Calm. Except for the cloud of smoke that had engulfed the car. Stinky tire smoke. A check of the mirror. Total darkness. A suck of air, much-needed air. I placed the car in first gear and slowly let the clutch pedal out as I headed down the front straight. I had gone past pit entrance. Though backwards, at 160 miles per hour.

"Ted," I said, taking a deep breath.

"Yeah?"

"I'll take you up on those rain tires."

"Yeah, come in this lap. What happened out there?"

"You don't want to know."

"Hit anything?"

"Nope – entering the back straight," I said into the radio.

"Rick is going to get in and bring it home to the finish," Ted informed me.

"Good." I couldn't wait to get out of this thing and go check my underwear.

I brought the Porsche down pit lane for the last time and helped Rick get in.

"Everything's great, go get 'em," I said as I slapped the top of his helmet, put up the window net, and slammed the door closed.

My knees were weak. It felt like I was going to be sick. I could barely lift my legs over the pit wall. Someone reached for me from behind and helped me into the pits. I made my way behind the pits and looked for a place to sit as I swallowed hard, pushing against the bile coming up my throat. I took a deep breath. My stomach was turning, not so much at the thought of hurting myself by crashing into that wall backwards at a hundred-plus miles per hour as at the thought of how screwed up the car could have been and how pissed and disappointed the crew would have been.

The next hour was perhaps the most stressful of my life. Only I knew what I had done to that poor race car. I had just twisted it and wrung its neck till its tongue hung out the grill. Was it going to break while we were solidly in the top five? Please, God, don't let it break. I knew I wouldn't be able to live with myself if we didn't finish because of me.

Rick brought the Commercial Motorsport Porsche home in fifth place. After twelve hours of hell we beat seventy-nine other teams. Everyone was very pleased with our performance. Considering the company we were in, a top five was not bad.

"So, what happened out there?" Rick asked me as I leaned against the trailer drinking a well-deserved beer.

"You don't want to know, but you might want to check the transmission," I said.

17

BE REASONABLE – DO IT MY WAY

With each new day Rick seemed much more attentive. He spent a lot of time looking at the TV, though I was not sure if he understood anything he saw or heard. He was definitely becoming more interested in what was going on around him. He had yet to say a word but was awake and alert for longer and longer periods of time.

The requests to visit were coming in at a steady pace. Rick was still in no shape to be taking visitors so we left the no visitation policy in place.

When Cathy and I got to his room one morning during this time, we were surprised to see that Bob Marshall and his wife, Marlene, were in the room. Bob had towed Rick's race trailer around for several years. But Bob was much more than a truck driver. He and Marlene would stay for the race on weekends and work on the team at various levels. Our family has known Bob for years. In fact Bob knew Dad long before Rick and I were even around. Dad knew him through his truck repair business.

Bob sat on a chair at the end of Rick's bed. He greeted me with a shocked look when I walked in. He got up and walked toward me as if he needed someone to talk to. Out in the hall, he told me his story.

"I walked in the room and then straight back out," he started. "Then I went back to the nurses' desk and asked them what room

Rick Bye was in and they told me 1105. I told them they were wrong. I can't believe it. I didn't recognize him."

Bob and Marlene stayed for about an hour. A very uncomfortable hour, which confirmed for us that we had made the right decision in closing visitation. Rick didn't need anyone seeing him in that condition. And vice versa.

After Bob and Marlene left I went straight back to the nurses' desk and reminded them that visitation was closed. They apologized and told me they would do their best to run interference.

One of many calls on my voicemail that day was from Blanche at Wawanessa Insurance. She said it was important.

"How is Rick?" she asked when I got through to her.

"Well, he's not very good," I said. "I'm really looking forward to getting him into rehab."

"Chris, that's what I wanted to talk to you about. There seems to be a bit of a problem. The day rates at the rehab facility down there are more than what our guidelines allow us to pay. I don't know if I can get Rick into the rehab center down there. We may have to bring him home where the day rates are more in line with ..."

"You mean cheaper," I said. "Blanche, listen to me. You and everyone at Wawanessa have been great. Don't change that now. Do whatever you have to do to get Rick into rehab down here. He's not coming home. Do you understand me, Blanche?"

She said she would give me a call a little later.

Now I was pissed. It wasn't that I was worried about the quality of the rehab in Canada. It was just that I knew that in Canada, as soon as Rick was somewhere between a root and a celery stock, they would throw him out of rehab. One of my father's employees had a massive accident at home a few months earlier, suffering head injuries. After a long hospital stay in Hamilton he was moved to a hospital in St. Catharines with no rehab facility. His wife got a call one day telling her that John was being transferred to a hospital in St. Catharines. She objected and reminded the person on the phone that the hospital there had no rehab facility. She was told that they were aware of this fact but he was still being moved. There were other people who needed his bed worse than he did.

That's the problem with the health-care system in Canada, as far as I can see. The country has great hospitals filled with great doctors and nurses. And closed beds, because there's not enough funding to keep them open.

After another very long day at the hospital we called it a day and headed for the Hawthorn. The days were getting longer and longer with each sunrise. They all seemed to run together. No day, no night, just one long constant struggle.

I walked into Ted's room at the Hawthorn.

"Want a drink?" he asked.

"No, I've got some beer, thanks," I said. I knew that a drink to him meant vodka. I drink beer only.

"Well," I said, not really meaning anything.

Ted just nodded. He does that a lot. Nodding is some kind of Bye family trait, along with mumbling. At least that's what we've been told many times.

"Remember the race at Mosport between us and Vic Sifton?" I asked him, trying to get our minds back to happier times.

"Yeah, I sure do," Ted said.

— — —

We were at Mosport in 1995 during a round of the Canadian Endurance Road Racing Championship. This was a new series that was founded by Rick after the Canadian Firestone Firehawk Championship folded in Canada. There was some political shuffling going on in Canadian motorsport in the mid-1990s and Rick was right in the middle of the shuffling. For some time it appeared there wasn't going to be any endurance racing in Canada. This would have been a major problem for Rick because that was the only way he made a living. In fact it was the only way for him to be himself.

Rick had called at the last minute, which was normal for him, to ask if I wanted to drive with him at the next round of the championship. I jumped at the opportunity, which was normal for me. A large part of my decision, though, was that Ted was going to be our crew chief again.

We qualifed on the front row and beside us was the Canaska Racing Porsche driven by Vic Sifton and Doug Beatty. Vic was the owner of Canaska Racing and one of their many drivers. He was known to have helped many Canadian race drivers at various levels.

Canaska had become a powerhouse on the Canadian racing scene, winning championships in pretty much every series they ran in. They were also a powerhouse in Formula Atlantic, with David Empringham as their number one driver. Some say David has more talent in his pinky finger than most drivers have in their whole bodies. Canaska was also a threat to win the World Challenge series with Richard Spenard at the wheel of their super hi-tech Camaro.

It was a great honor and accomplishment to qualify on the front row with such a prestigious team, particularly when they were much better funded than we were.

Ted and I were walking on the front straight at Mosport as the cars were being staged before the start of the race. Rick was preparing to start the Commercial Motorsport KFC Porsche 968, and Doug Beatty was in the Canaska Porsche for the first stint of the two-hour race. There were about thirty cars lined up on the front straight, and I was relishing the noise and the smells. I walked around the KFC Porsche and stuck my hand in through the window net to give Rick a quick squeeze on the shoulder. He just gave me a slight nod.

The green flag dropped and going into turn 1 first was Beatty, closely followed by Rick. About a minute and a half later we heard the field coming, Beatty and Bye in the two leading Porsches, with the rest of the field in tow. Camaros, Firebirds, Nissans, Mustangs, and of course more Porsches went screaming by, bumper to bumper, just inches from the pit wall. *SSSHEWW, SSSHEW, SSSHEW, SSSHEW.*

Ted was standing beside the pit wall with his headset on. He was in constant communication with all the drivers on the Commercial Motorsport team. In this race our team was made up of two cars and four drivers. Ted was always great to have on the radio because he never said much. But when he did say something, you had better be listening. Whatever he had to say could win you the race.

The race settled into a fast and steady pace with the green Canaska Porsche leading the red and white Commercial Motorsport KFC Porsche. I was pacing in the pit except for the odd trip to the pit wall. I find being in the pits much more nerve-wracking than being in the race car. As I stood in the pit stall, Ted caught my eye and gave me a quick nod to get ready.

A strange calmness set in as it always does when I'm told it's time to get going. I took a deep breath and picked up my helmet. I took my balaclava and gloves out of my helmet and set them back down. I pulled the balaclava over my head and struggled to locate the eye holes. I pulled on my helmet and the world around me went quiet. After doing up my helmet strap I put my gloves on and then turned and faced Ted and waited for him to look at me. We made eye contact and nothing needed to be said. Ted knew I was ready and eager to get into the KFC Porsche. I stepped back out of the way of the crew and stood waiting, calmly, for the approaching storm.

When you're waiting to get into a race car when it's running a strong second it's important not to think of certain things, such as: If I crash the car the crew is going to be some pissed, all twenty of them. If I crash the car, it will be expensive. Crashing was something Rick and I never talked about. Fortunately it was never an issue. I was just lucky that way.

"This lap," everyone in the pits started to yell. Ted looked across pit lane and directly at me. I gave him a quick nod.

"Deep breath," I said to myself as my heart rate started climbing.

Beatty brought the Canaska Porsche slowly past us and down pit lane. The Canaska guys were pitted at the far end of pit lane and we were at the very first pit. Rick brought the KFC Porsche into pit lane and immediately to a stop in our pit. I looked down pit lane as I jumped over the wall. The Canaska car hadn't even made it to their pit yet.

Beautiful, I thought as I ran around the front of the car and the entire team swarmed the car like bees on honey.

Once the driver exchange was complete everyone yelled at once *go, go, go*. The car was in first gear with the rear wheels spinning. I quickly got to the sixty kilometers per hour, the pit lane speed limit, and locked my eyes on the green Porsche that had been leading the field for the whole race.

I could see that they had yet to complete their pit stop as ours got started much sooner because we were at the near end of pit lane. I could see Beatty talking to Sifton who had just got in. I was confident I could beat Vic, but I knew he had had a lot of seat time lately.

There was never a time when I wanted to speed more than right then. At that very moment Rick came on the radio: "60K, 60K is the pit lane speed limit. *Do not* get a stop and go."

"10-4," I replied.

The trip down pit lane is painfully slow. Looking at the car that has been leading the whole race only makes it more painful. I am going to beat them out of the pits, I said to myself as I got closer and closer to their pit.

"We've got them," I said, then, more quietly, "Damn," as they dropped the car off the stands and smoke came off the rear tires. We left the pit lane literally attached. I have a habit of making myself known to anyone who happens to be in front of me by attaching myself to the rear of their car. I didn't know whether I could force Vic into making a mistake, but I sure was going to try. We slid out of pit lane and into turn 1. Both cars were extremely loose due to some eight new race tires. New tires tend to be very slick until you can get some temperature in them.

"Okay, Vic, here we go, let's see what you're made of," I yelled into my helmet.

I stayed right on Vic's tail until we got to the back straight, where he pulled me by a couple of car lengths. It was becoming apparent that the Canaska Porsche was more than equal to ours. A couple of car lengths may not sound like much, but believe me it, can be an eternity if the advantage isn't yours.

As we came off the back straight I started to reel Vic back in. He was messing up corner 9 real bad. I wasn't sure if he just screwed it up in this one lap or if he wasn't very fast there in general. I made my mind up to follow him and see where he was fast and where I was faster. I settled into a comfortable pace and stayed within a car length of him.

"Make sure I know when the last lap is coming," I said to Ted on the radio.

"No problem," he replied. "Everything okay?"

"Just fine," I said, knowing we could win this thing.

For the next hour I followed Vic's Porsche. I could smell the exhaust. Like a cougar stalking an antelope, I knew exactly where and when I was going to pounce.

"Chris, I think the last-lap board should come out this lap," Ted said.

"Got it," I replied.

Coming up the back straight, Vic pulled me by a couple of car lengths, just as he had been doing the entire stint. As we came into corner 8 I quickly reeled him in, leaving the braking for corner 9 way later than normal. Vic screwed up corner 9 just as he had every lap since I followed him out of the pits. I shot past him by about ten miles per hour. I glanced in the mirror as I turned into corner 10. Vic was four or five car lengths back. Perfect. As I exited corner 10 I looked up and saw the official starter with the last-lap sign in his hand. Ted was right, this was the last lap, and the next thing I hoped to see was the starter throwing the checkered flag. I just hoped I would see it before anyone else.

As I flew down the front straight, Ted and Rick were leaning over the pit wall just staring. I prepared to enter corner 1 at about a hundred miles per hour and decided to check my mirrors once again. I still had about a four-car length lead on Vic. Perfect, I thought again ... and completely missed the turn in point for corner 1.

Something strange comes over you when you get into trouble in a race car. Things seem to go into slow motion. I turned the car to the right, knowing I was in big trouble. The back of the car started to rotate to the left as I tried desperately to get the front of the car to the apex. Now the car was in a complete four-wheel slide toward the guardrail. For some reason you never think to yourself, "This is going to hurt," but you probably should. As the rear wheels got closer to the outside curb, I stood on the throttle for all I was worth. The car made some strange sounds, kind of like grunts. It slowly, very slowly, started to go in the direction of the track. I kept my eyes focused down the road. I knew that was the only thing that would save me, if anything could.

The left-side tires climbed up onto the speed curbing, the red and white curbs placed throughout corners on racetracks. Then they slid off the curbs and onto the grass on the other side of the track. Now I was officially screwed, with two wheels on the track and two wheels on the grass at well over a hundred miles per hour. I have seen so many people write cars off at the exit of corner 1 at Mosport by trying to get back on the track too fast. I knew if I was to get out of this mess and back on track, I would have to do it very gently.

It worked. Out of my right-side peripheral, I saw the nose of Victor's Porsche. He had taken complete advantage of my misfortune, or more accurately stupidity, just as any race-car driver would do.

As we approached corner 2, Vic was halfway up the right side of my car and only an inch or two from trading paint. Just before the top of the hill, I started to move Vic to the right. Thankfully, he complied as I got closer to him. And as we crested the hill I went straight instead of turning left.

As you approach corner 2 at Mosport you go slightly uphill. Over the crest of the hill the road turns 90 degrees to the left. It is also somewhat off camber – it's banked, but banked the wrong way. Blind, off camber, no run-off area, and blindingly fast, fourth gear in most cars, well over a hundred miles per hour, that's corner 2. Some of the world's best race-car drivers, including former world champion Jackie Stewart, have said the corner is one of the most difficult of any racetrack in the world. The last place you want to be is on the outside of another car at the top of the corner, especially if that other car has decided not to turn. This forces you off line and out into the shit, the dirt, rock, and pieces of racing tires on the outside of the corner.

Vic did just what I expected him to do: he lifted off the throttle. I was on line and this allowed me to get a bit of a run into corner 3. I needed to really put my head down and put some distance between my car and his before we got to the back straight. Vic could pull me up the hill on the back straight. I needed to have four or five car lengths on him before we got there and I only had two corners to do it. I nailed corner 3 flat on the throttle at the apex and pulled away from Vic just a bit more. Then it was time for corner 4.

This corner is a dauntingly fast left-hand, downhill, 90-degree corner that can be done flat out in a pretty much any formula car, but not in most sedans. That is, unless it's a Porsche. Deep breath, right on line, no lift, flat out over the top of the hill. This takes your breath away, but do it right and you feel like you and the car are flying. The rear of the car drifts a little to the right as you get to the bottom of the hill. It's important to keep the car as close to the left side of the road at the exit of the corner because the next corner is a right hander.

To be precise, a second-gear, 50 mph right hander. I was flat in fourth gear at about 110. I had sixty or seventy feet to get this thing slowed down.

The brake rotors glowed as I stood on the brake pedal as hard as I could. The car had ABS and, as always, we had it turned on. We always run a switch on the ABS system so we can turn it off if we want to. The car began to slow down fast, but not enough to make the corner. I turned in, still hard on the brakes. This caused the car to rotate to the left. Just as the car was pointed where I wanted it, I slammed the throttle back down. Off the gas and turn into corner 5B. This corner is a two-part corner, 5A and 5B. 5B leads onto the back straight. I slammed the throttle back down abruptly as I turned into 5B, hit the apex, and accelerated up the back straight. Now it was time to check the mirrors. Vic was a good six or seven car lengths back.

Up the back straight I stayed close to the right side of the road. This would force Vic to try going around my left side. The corner off the back straight is corner 8. No one really knows where corners 6 and 7 are. Since Vic had to try to pass me on my left side, he had to go the long way around when we got to corner 8. If he got up beside me when it came time to turn in, I was quite prepared to go straight once again and push him into the shit. Vic never quite made it up beside me. I led into corner 8 and through 9 and 10. Out of 10, I throttled hard against the firewall, my heart pounding against the tight seatbelts.

As I crossed the finish line in first, Rick and Ted stood at the pit wall smiling. I looked over to the pits as I screamed in my radio and the entire crew was going apeshit. I could see them jumping up and down screaming with their hands in the air. This is why I love this sport so much, I thought. There is nothing better than winning a motor race, and there is nothing more frustrating than finishing second, especially after leading a good part of it.

I pulled into victory circle and the crew was running around hugging everyone in sight. Rick and Ted stood back in their calm, cool way and just looked over at me with their half grins. Rick just nodded when we made eye contact.

18
A FISH STORY

Communicating with Rick was slow and tedious. None of us knew exactly when we began to communicate with him because it started out so slowly. It wasn't like he just woke up one day and started talking. That happens in some coma cases, but certainly not in ours. It started with Rick just looking and focusing. We would call his name and he would slowly turn his head and look in our direction, sometimes. When he did look in your direction it was a flip of a coin whether he was going to look at you. And then it was another 50/50 whether or not he focused on you. This went on for weeks, and by now it was late February.

After he was consistently focusing on us when we spoke to him, the next thing he did was open his eyes as wide as he could while at the same time raising his eyebrows, not unlike a dog tilting its head when you talk to it. He did this every time we spoke to him, and this stage seemed to go on forever. When we wanted a yes answer, we would unconsciously nod our heads up and down and say yes. Rick then gradually started to nod his head up and down to our questions.

"Are you hungry?" Eyebrows up, eyes wide open, and a nod up and then down.

"Are you thirsty?" Eyebrows up, eyes wide open, and a nod up and then down.

"Do you want a beer?" Eyebrows up, eyes wide open, and a nod up and then down.

He has never drunk beer in his life.

Every day he seemed to make a step in the direction of progress, a very small step. Or perhaps a partial step is more accurate. Rick eventually segued from these nods to mouthing words, or more like just moving his lower jaw up and down just like his nods. Like an infant, he was learning to imitate what he was seeing. According to the people around me, this was good, but I was far from convinced.

Eventually Rick started to make very slow, very quiet sounds. Then he slowly started to form words. His voice was quiet and raspy. It looked like it hurt him to talk, physically and mentally. He had to concentrate, with eyes wide open and eyebrows up, on each and every word before he attempted to get it to come out. And they came out one word at a time, followed by several seconds of the eyebrow routine. As days turned into weeks, Rick's speech came along slowly, like a steam roller.

This was hard for me to watch. However, he was going in the right direction because he hadn't taken a step backwards since he started to talk or, more accurately, to rasp.

The doctors in the ICU had told us it was common for someone who had suffered such a head injury to wake up as a very different person. In fact, with their help we went through a grieving process to say goodbye to the old person and prepare to say hello to the new one. The doctors led us through this process, telling us that he would have no control over who he would be when he came to. They also gave us some hope that this did not happen in every head injury case.

Once he started talking he might say some inappropriate things, they said. One of them recalled an ordained priest who woke up and swore like a trucker. "Hey nurse, get your ass over here and fill up my water," he would say at full volume without a clue that he was saying anything wrong. When they asked him not to use such language, he just looked confused.

They also prepared us for the fact that it was common for people coming out of a coma to touch inappropriately, as in groping the nurses. They told us not to worry – the nurses were aware of these things and knew how to handle such situations.

With Rick, there was no problem with swearing, but he did become very touchy-feely with the nurses. He wasn't aggressive, he just touched their arms, or more accurately stroked their arms, whenever he had a chance. He seemed to know what he could and could not get away with. He never touched any of the nurses where he shouldn't. Strangely, he never touched Mom or Cathy in this way, even though he had no clue who they were.

A couple of weeks after Rick had started with the eyebrow raising, his speech became a lot clearer. It would be another several days before he would start to ask questions rather than answer them. None of us was prepared for the questions we were about to get.

I walked into Rick's room and he was just lying on the bed with his eyes closed. I was not sure if he was sleeping or gliding out in space somewhere. It was kind of a crapshoot what kind of state he would be in when you walked into his room.

I sat down in a chair in the corner and prepared to read a book. Rick slowly opened his eyes. But his eyes didn't do what you would expect when someone just wakes up. Most people, when they wake up, slowly turn their head one way and then the other. Rick just opened his eyes and stared straight at the ceiling. No blinking, no eye movement, no turning of his head, nothing, just a blank stare.

In time Rick finally turned and looked over at me. "Hey, man, come here for a sec," he said in his now familiar raspy whisper.

I got up and walked over to the bed.

He slowly looked down and tried to pull his blanket aside. "You need to do me a favor," he said.

"Yeah, sure, what's up?"

"Can you go to the kitchen and get me a knife?"

"A knife? What do you want a knife for?"

"Here, take a look at my knee," he said as he tried to pull the blanket aside again. I helped him uncover his right knee. That knee had been swelling, badly, and the doctors didn't seem to have an answer for it. It wasn't at the top of their minds, which made sense given all of the other issues we were dealing with.

I saw that his knee was swollen to the size of a large grapefruit. Rick looked down at it and then back up to me. He started to tell me the story of his knee. And what a story it was.

"Okay," he said. "They took me into the operating room the other day and they did an operation. They cut my knee open and put three fish in there. I told them that they should go in and take them out but they just ignored me. They don't listen!" His eyes moved slowly from his knee to my eyes. "You have got to go to the kitchen and get me a knife so I can take the fish out. They're killing me. My knee really hurts."

"Fish?"

"Yeah, three, there are three fish in my knee!"

"Three," I said, staring into his vacant eyes. "I don't think it would be a good idea to try to take the fish out yourself, do you?"

"Well, I asked them and they won't do it. I don't think they believe me," he said.

No shit, Einstein.

"I'll go down the kitchen and see if I can find a knife," I said and walked into the hallway.

Okay, where are we? Where are we going? I didn't have a clue. Was this better or was this worse? What is he going to be? Who is he going to be? What am I going to be? What is our family going to be? Who is our family going to be when this all ends? How will it end? Fish? Fish in your knee?

I was hoping if I told him I was going to get a knife and didn't come back for a while he would just forget where I was going. Luckily, I was right. But this would not be the last time we would hear about the fish. They were to become the subject of many conversations, with and without Rick.

— — —

"We think he's ready to go into the Sticht Center," the therapist said later that day, looking at Rick asleep in his bed. The center was a rehab facility, attached to the hospital, that had been open for less than a year.

"So what will he be doing differently in there from here?" I asked.

"Oh, a lot. Would you like to come over and take a tour?"

We arranged to meet in Rick's room the next morning at 9.

At the appointed hour, the therapist took my parents and Cathy and me down in the elevator to the basement. This was the one part of the hospital none of us had been in before. A tunnel was built from the hospital to the rehab center so patients wouldn't have to be taken outside during transfer. Once at the other end of the tunnel, we entered the lobby area of the Sticht Center and then went up in the elevator to a floor that Rick would soon call home.

This place struck me as very different from the hospital. It didn't have a hospital feel. I guess it had a rehab feel, whatever that is.

Our tour guide was the head nurse on the head injury floor. An entire floor dedicated to head injuries. And it was impressive. She explained that the floor had a total of twelve beds. The rooms were much bigger than Rick's current room. It also had a full gym.

The gym was very impressive. And there was a piece of equipment I'd never seen in a gym before. Right there in the middle of the gym was a Chrysler K car. Some might say a gym is a much better place for a K car than a road.

"What's with the car?" I asked.

The nurse told us that the patients practiced getting into and out of the car, which made the transition back to their real lives a lot easier.

The nurse then went into what Rick's day would look like once he was transferred. Every patient gets a 7 a.m. wake-up call, she said. Breakfast is served at 7:30. Rehab starts at 8 and goes till 4 in the afternoon, with an hour for lunch.

We all looked at each other. Nothing much needed to be said, because we were all thinking the same thing: that this place was awesome and that Rick needed to be here right now.

"Okay, when can we move him in?" I asked the head nurse.

"Well, that's not up to me. You will have to work with the people in administration on that."

— — —

Bob Carlson called and wondered if he and Bob Paterson could visit Rick.

I was not about to deny Rick – or me – this pleasure.

Bob Paterson was a left-handed relief pitcher for the Chicago Cubs. Rick and Bob Carlson met him when Porsche did an event for the Cubs at their spring training camp in Phoenix. Porsche had been in Phoenix launching the all-new Boxster at Phoenix International Raceway, and they invited the Cubs over to the track on one of their days off. Porsche is always thinking of ways to get the right people into their cars, and who could be more right than the Chicago Cubs?

"Absolutely, Bob, you guys are welcome any time," I said. "Give me a call when you get to the hospital."

When they came in for the visit I told them I needed to prepare them a little before they went in. "He is somewhat confused and says some pretty strange things at times. He may or may not know who you are so just kind of go along with what he has to say. He has lost a lot of weight and he doesn't look very good."

I decided to let them have a few minutes to themselves with Rick before I went in.

Bob and Bob were not saying anything when I walked in. Bob Paterson was looking out the window. Bob Carlson looked up at me in the doorway, clearly shaken.

Rick was sitting in his Lazy Boy chair in the corner of the room. Well, he wasn't really sitting. He always started out that way but then he would slowly slide down the chair toward the floor. He didn't have the strength, ability, or sense to pull himself up. He looked so helpless in this position, so pathetic.

"Well, we're going to get going," Bob Carlson said to Rick, looking over at him even though it was clear he had to force himself to do so.

"Okay, thanks for coming," Rick said in a slow, mumbled whisper, unsure who he was saying goodbye to.

I saw Bob and Bob to the elevator, Bob Carlson wasn't doing too well. He and Rick had a very tight relationship and Bob was just an all round good guy and caring friend. Bob Paterson and I spoke briefly about getting together during spring training in Phoenix. I had plans to go there for an Audi program during that time.

When I went back into Rick's room he was asleep. Or was he? He had his eyes closed, but what did that mean? Sometimes when his eyes were open he wasn't awake. So did that mean when his eyes closed he *was* awake? I told Mom and Cathy that I was pretty much spent and was thinking of calling it a day.

19
GETTING WORSE, MUCH WORSE

"Hey, man, how you doin'?" I asked Rick the next morning as I entered his room.

"Okay, how are you?" he replied. "Do you know where she went?"

I looked at Mom and Cathy. They shrugged their shoulders.

"Who?" I asked.

"The girl who was just here," Rick said.

"Girl, what girl? There wasn't any girl here."

"Yeah, she just left," he said, with a hint of frustration. He turned his head toward the television and then slowly back to me.

"Where was this girl when you last saw her?"

"There," Rick said as he looked back toward the TV.

A woman had walked off screen and he thought she was in the room. What next? Cathy gave me a half smile. I wondered if she knew that I was getting worse as Rick was getting better.

Administration told me they wanted to get Rick into the rehab center but that there was a problem with the insurance company. The day rate – $1,000 – was higher than what the company was willing to pay.

I called the company and asked for Blanche.

"We have toured the Sticht Center," I told her, "and I know you have talked to the hospital about getting him in there."

"Chris, as I said, the rates down there are much higher than what we pay," she said.

"I don't care, Blanche. Just make it happen I can't imagine you're going to save any money if we ship him to someplace in Ontario and he ends up spending twice as much time there. You really need to make this happen."

I told her not to take it personally but that I was not taking no for an answer.

On top of all this, Rick was convinced he was in Mt. Tremblant.

"Have you seen Vince lately?" he asked me in his slow steady voice.

"Vince?"

"Yeah, Vince. You know, something really weird is going on."

His mind seemed to be drifting away from Vince, at least for a time.

"Yeah, what's that?"

"Well, everyone around here keeps telling me that I'm in North Carolina. I don't know why they insist on telling me that when they know I'm in Mt. Tremblant."

That explained the Vince thing. Vince is the track manager at Le Circuit Mt. Tremblant racetrack.

"Rick, we are in North Carolina. Winston-Salem, North Carolina. Why do you think we are in Tremblant?"

"Oh. You, too. Why are you on their side?"

"Rick, I'm on your side. Everyone is on your side."

He turned his head and looked out the window.

"I don't know – he just started talking about being in Mt. Tremblant," Mom told me later outside his room.

"Well, I don't think it really matters much," I said. "It's probably best if we don't argue with him. It seems to upset him. If he thinks he's in Tremblant, then let's let him think that."

– – –

All this talk about Tremblant reminded me of one of our adventures there, one I hoped Rick would remember someday when he knew where he really was.

It was 1989 and we were in the ski town for another round of the Porsche Advanced Driving School. Mt. Tremblant, one of the most beautiful places on earth, is located about one and a half hours north of Montreal. The racetrack we were using for the weekend was Le Circuit Mt. Tremblant, without a doubt one of the most picturesque racetracks on earth.

We were all staying at Cuttles Resort, situated on the side of a large hill that ended abruptly at the shore of a fairly large lake. There were several condo buildings placed at different levels along the hillside. The building located nearest the lake was the registration building and bar. Our weekend would officially begin with a cocktail reception in the bar.

A bunch of us had come together from Toronto in Hank's van. Hank drove and Lenny, Peter, and I came along for the ride. We went with him for two reasons. One was to keep Hank company on the eight-hour drive, and the other was so we didn't have to drive. Hank would get pissed when he stopped for gas and couldn't get any of us to take the wheel. He would ask and we would all say, at the same time, no thanks.

As usual we had a few beers during the day while our guests arrived and checked in. Some of the guys went down to the lake and just hung out. Others went over to the track, which was only a mile or so away. Everyone knew we had to be in the bar for cocktails at 7 p.m. As a bunch of us instructors went down the walkway toward the bar, we all came to a screeching halt. There in the middle of forty or fifty new Porsches was a trailer behind a Chevy Suburban with something on it that looked very much like a Porsche race car under a cover.

"What the hell is that?" someone asked.

"I have no idea, but I do know one thing for sure: it doesn't belong to any of my students," I said matter of factly.

"Yeah, mine neither," Peter said, laughing.

Once at the cocktail party we all headed straight to Hank. "Okay, what's up with the race car in the parking lot?" we whispered to him as we scanned the room trying to figure out who it belonged to.

"I have no idea, but I'm about to find out," Hank said.

We all grabbed a drink and then wandered around the room chatting with our guests, trying to find out who owned the thing. We asked everyone we talked to what they were driving. All we heard was 928, 911, 911 Turbo, 944, 944 Turbo.

During the cocktail party Lenny said to the rest of us, "Hey, let's go down to Le Falcon Bleu for one."

"One," Peter said with a smirk.

"Well, okay, maybe two or three."

And off eight or ten of us went.

Le Falcon Bleu was not one of Quebec's more fashionable locations. It was, well, let's just say it was a shoe show. That's a place where the ladies show off their shoes – and not much else.

I have no idea how long we sat there before the door opened and lo and behold, in walked Hank with Michael Ney in tow. Michael was the boss.

I don't think the door had even closed behind them before Lenny called over one of the performers and sent her over to Hank and Michael. Next thing we knew, we saw the two men walking out the door.

"Aw, come on, chicken," someone yelled at Hank as we were all laughing our asses off.

It was very late when someone reminded us we had a 6 a.m. wake-up call. There was a fight over who would drive – none of us wanted to. As we left the bar, I stopped at the restroom because I had to once again empty my thimble-sized bladder. When I stepped outside, every seat in the van was taken except the driver's.

"Okay, morons, I don't want to drive," I said.

"Too bad, loser," Lenny responded, with an undeniable level of attitude. I had thought this might happen so I had cooled it on the drinks earlier in the night.

So off we went, back to Cuttles. My condo was in the highest complex, the one farthest from the lake. The edge of the parking lot faced the lake and the mountains on the far side. Everyone was pretty much knackered at this point, as Rick would say, meaning half asleep.

"Well, I'm home," I said quietly, stopping the van in the middle of the parking lot of my condo complex. Without putting the van into park, I opened the door and slipped into the night. The van slowly rolled toward the edge of the parking lot where it quickly turned into a long steep grassy slope heading straight to the lake.

"Asshole," everyone screamed amid a flurry of grunts and groans as every single guy in the van scrambled to get into the driver's seat.

The van continued to roll, gaining speed. As I opened the door of my condo, I thought, I guess I don't have to worry about them making me drive anymore.

The next morning, which by the way was only about three hours after we got home, every single guy in that van gave me the same look as they walked into breakfast. A look of amazement at what I had done, along with a grin. Even they had to admit it was pretty damn funny.

We finished breakfast, gathered up our stuff, and headed for the track. We would normally show up an hour or so before the guests. As we got the track set up, the Porsches started to arrive, a sight that I never get sick of, forty, fifty, or sixty shiny new Porsches. How could anyone not enjoy looking at that?

Along with all of the new Porsches came the truck, the Suburban with the mystery car under the cover. We all walked over to see just what the hell was on this trailer. The driver of the truck got out and slowly started to remove the cover as he said hello to his audience. We all stared as first the nose, then the windshield, roof, and finally the tail came into view.

"What the hell is that?" I whispered to Peter.

"I have no clue. I'm just glad he's your student," he replied as he took a long slow puff on his pipe.

"Mine?"

Peter then broke into his unmistakable and great laugh.

Under the cover was what appeared to be a full-blown 935 Porsche race car. The owner then started to tell us all about it, the heritage, horsepower, and torque.

Okay, where was this guy's street car? The program wasn't designed for race cars. What was this guy doing here anyhow?

After we watched him unload his car, we walked up to the restaurant where everyone had gathered for coffee and to learn from Hank just what their day would look like. As a group we asked Hank what was up with the race car in the parking lot.

"I'm still trying to find out," he assured us.

The way the Porsche Advanced Driving School worked, the students were split into three groups. The groups would then grab their cars and go to different areas of the track to start different exercises.

The groups would stand beside their cars and wait for the instructors to come up and introduce themselves. On this occasion every car had left pit lane except for one: yep, you guessed it, the race-car dude.

Two of us instructors were left hiding behind the timing tower, Paul Lambke and me. "Paul, I'm going to take a break for the first session, so why don't you take that guy?" I said.

"Yeah, sure," he said, walking down pit lane and giving me one of those kiss-my-ass looks.

I walked along a little behind Paul as he introduced himself to the owner of the race car. The guy shook Paul's hand and then started to climb into the car. Paul walked around to the passenger side and opened the door. He looked over the roof of the car directly at me and rolled his eyes. I walked around and looked into the car.

I quickly saw what the eye rolling was all about. Inside this Porsche was a passenger seat, although it looked like someone had put it in the night before. There was a full roll cage in the interior, complete with a fire system. The right-side front leg of the roll cage came right across the center of the front seat and rested across the front of it.

Paul put his helmet on and then put his left leg in first as he straddled the roll cage. He then let his butt slide down into the seat and his right leg was now in the car, but on the other side of the roll cage. I helped him get his seat belts done up, closed the door, and inserted the door pin that many race cars have. I looked in through the windshield and gave Paul a big smile and the old thumbs-up signal. The driver finished wrestling with his safety harness and seat adjustments and finally settled in. Then he reached for the dash, which like most race cars had a start button.

RUNT, RUNT, RUNT, the engine went as it turned over, slowly. For a minute it looked like it wasn't going to start. If Paul could have got out on his own, he would have already started to do so.

RUNT, RUNT, RUNT, BLAT, BLAT, BLAT, BLAH, BLAH, BLAH, RENT, RENT, RENT, the engine howled as the driver toggled away on the throttle. It was so loud you couldn't hear yourself think. Someone in pit lane gave the driver the all clear sign.

RENT, RENT, REEEENT, REEEENT, BLAT ... Dead quiet ... He had stalled it. Paul was now looking out the side window for someone to come to his rescue.

RUNT, RUNT, RUNT, BLAT, BLAT, BLAT, REEEEENT, REEEEE, BLAH, BLAH, BLAH, the car went as the driver finally got the clutch out and headed the car down pit lane.

He took the car up through the gears with the back wheels spinning most of the way out of the pits. I was killing myself laughing, over what poor Paul was going through.

The quiet was broken by the sounds of this 600-horsepower monster approaching. The car went up through Nammarow, a corner leading onto the front straight. We heard the guy hard on the throttle as he left the corner. *REEEEEEEEEEEEEN,* the car went as it zoomed down the front straight and into corner 1.

"Where the hell is Lambke?" someone asked. He seemed to have disappeared under the dash.

"Perhaps he made the guy stop and he got out," I said.

We were standing in pit lane as we waited to watch the next lap. No noise, no sound. Finally we saw the race car come idling down pit lane with its engine off.

"Perfect. It broke," I said.

The car came to a rolling stop just past us. We saw the top of Lambke's head start to move around as we walked up and unpinned the passenger door. Paul rolled out of the door and slowly walked up to me.

"I don't fit. He needs somebody short to go with him," he said.

"What the hell you looking at me for?" I said, pointing out that he is about five feet four and I was five nine.

Paul simply turned and walked away, leaving me standing in pit lane alone. The driver of the race car was looking at me in his mirror, wondering what was going on.

Damn, Lambke, I am going to kill you!

I grabbed my helmet and walked toward the car. I slid my left leg under the roll bar as my ass hit the seat. With my right leg hooked over the roll bar I felt I should be arrested for what I was doing to it.

The driver looked over at me and said, "Ready?"

"Yeah, sure," I said after doing up my safety belt.

RUNT, RUNT, RUNT, went the engine as it slowly turned over. *BLAT, BLAT, BLAT,* it screamed as it came to life. The driver looked at me and moved his lower jaw up and down.

BLAT, BLAT, BLAT, was all that came out.

I smiled politely and nodded.

We screamed down pit lane at what seemed a hundred miles an hour. Second, third, *WAAAAAAAAAAAAAAAAAA* out of pit lane and into corner 1. I was straddling the roll cage and hanging on for all I was worth.

In most cars you're going flat out in top gear as you enter corner 1 at Le Circuit Mt. Tremblant. This guy was hard on the throttle and we were flying. As we got to the top of the right hander, the road quickly dropped out from underneath us. Just as we reached the top of the hill, the driver's door flew open.

As if that wasn't bad enough, he reached for the door. Here I was, strapped into a rocket ship with some guy I had never met and I had no idea of his skill level, if any, going over a hundred miles an hour and he was reaching for the door.

"Forget the door, just drive," I yelled at the top of my lungs as I reached for the steering wheel. He must have heard something because he looked over at me. He once again did that thing with his lower jaw.

Somehow we got through corners 1 and 2 without killing ourselves and we slowly headed for pit lane to get the driver's door pin put back in. At least that was what he thought. I just wanted out. As the car came to a stop, I jumped out and gave Hank a *your turn* look. Hank decided it was time to tell buddy we needed him to take his race car home and come back with the new 911 he had just bought. I think our boy racer was just as glad. He was as scared as we were. The next day he came back with his new car and enjoyed the day much more, and so did we.

– – –

I knew it was time to go back to work. I hadn't been at working for several weeks by now. I had to go to Arizona to do a job for Audi. Volkswagen and Audi have a proving grounds – an automotive test center – there. Besides, going to Arizona in February was always a good idea.

I arrived in Arizona on a Saturday and we didn't have to start setting up till the next day. The first place I headed from the airport was

Rubio's Baja Grill, for their world-famous fish tacos. You can't find fish tacos anywhere except in the Southwest.

It was a typical Arizona day, eighty degrees and dry. I was sitting on a patio outside the restaurant eating fish tacos and nachos with killer hot salsa and drinking a cold Bud. Boy, I needed this. I had no idea how long I was there, but after a couple more Buds, I went to my hotel and settled in for the night. I decided not to call home or the hospital. I knew Rick was in good hands.

The Chicago Cubs were in town for spring training and Bob Paterson and I had made plans to get together that week. They were playing the Pittsburgh Pirates on Sunday and Bob invited me to come out to the game as his guest. I had never been much of a baseball fan, but I was looking forward to spending a few hours watching and learning about the game. I knew the distraction would do me good.

My seat was right behind home plate. I settled in to enjoy the game and try to figure out what was going on. I picked up a little from the people around me, most of them players' wives.

The only time I saw Bob was when he was out by the outfield warming up. The Cubs' new pitcher, Kerry Wood, was on the mound. I had no idea how fast he was throwing the ball, but it was fast. I wondered how the hell you could even start to swing at something that comes at you at that speed. The batter must have to start his swing before the ball even left the mound. Finally, Bob walked out to the mound.

One, two, three pitches and one, two, three strikes. I cheered along with the rest of the crowd. The next thing I knew, Bob was walking off the field, replaced by Terry Mulholland.

What was that all about? Bob just threw three bombs and they took him out of the game.

I asked Bob about it in the dressing room after the game. He laughed as he explained to me that he as a left-handed relief pitcher he was often brought into the game to pitch against just one batter.

"So you get up there and do your job and that's it?" I asked.

"Yep, you got it."

Bob called Terry Mulholland over to meet me.

"Chris is Rick Bye's brother," Bob told him.

"So how is he?" Terry asked.

"Well, he's doing a lot better than he was at first," I said.

"Tell him I was asking about him," Terry said.

Bob and I decided to call Rick. Mom came on the line and said the insurance company had called again the night before.

"They wanted me to sign some more papers that they were going to fax over," she said. "I just don't know what to do."

"Mom, don't sign anything. In fact, don't even talk to them. If they call you again tell them to call me on my cell." I asked her to put Rick on.

"How are you doing?" I asked.

"Well, I'm a little confused," he said. "I can't figure out why they would give me ice cream for breakfast. It's really weird but no one else seems to think so."

"Yeah, that is a little weird," I said.

It was afternoon in Arizona so it was dinnertime at the hospital. This was just one of those things not worth arguing about with him. I wondered whether I was doing him any favors by not correcting him. He was difficult to deal with before he hit his head. Now he was impossible. "Hey, I'm here with Bob Paterson and he wants to talk to you," I said.

I looked at Bob and whispered, "He thinks it's morning. Just go with it."

"Hey, man, how are you doing?" Bob said. Then he grinned and said, "Yeah, that is kinda weird."

I reminded Mom not to talk to the insurance company and said goodbye.

"I love you," she said as we hung up, just has she had said at the end of every call since the accident. It isn't that we don't get along or love each other, it's just that we never said it to each other much before the accident. In fact, we never said it at all. I don't think I have ever told Rick that I loved him. Hell, we're professional race-car drivers, we're macho guys. Why the hell would we ever say that to each other?

I wondered if I would have regretted not telling him that I loved him if he hadn't made it out of the ER.

– – –

The trip back to Winston-Salem was long and tedious. I hate traveling from the west coast back to the east. No matter how you cut it, you lose a whole day.

I was looking forward to seeing Rick. Mom had been telling me all week how great he was doing. The only problem she mentioned was that he was still convinced he was in Mt. Tremblant. But that was no big deal. I was sure we would eventually convince him otherwise.

I walked into 1105 with a bounce in my step, possibly for the first time since the accident.

"Hey, man, how you doing?" I said before even looking to see who was in the room.

"Good, how are you?" Rick replied, in his slow raspy, faint, voice.

"Rick, do you know who this is?" Mom said out of the blue.

Rick slowly turned his head back toward the corner where she was sitting. It was painful watching his head turn. It appeared to be a huge effort for him to do this simple task. "Yeah," he replied.

"Who?" Mom asked.

It took him awhile, but he eventually turned toward me and stared straight into my eyes. I don't know how long he looked at me before the light bulb went off in his head and his eyes lit up. *Thank god,* I thought. I had been expecting so much before I walked into this room. It would have killed me if he didn't even know who I was.

Rick slowly turned his head back toward Mom with a confident, smartass grin. "My friend from South Carolina," he said proudly.

Mom's eyes were on me before Rick could get out the entire answer.

I don't know how long I stood there. I didn't move, didn't blink, didn't breathe. It felt as if I had been hit in the chest with a baseball bat. I struggled to get my breath. This was the most physical, non-physical shot I had ever taken. I don't remember looking at Mom or Rick, I just slowly backed out of the room. Once out in the hall I turned and started walking.

Through the fog in my head I heard the words, "Hey, you okay?" It was Amy Olson. "Are you okay?" she repeated as she grabbed my arm.

I looked at her, unable to speak. The lump in my throat was not only stopping me from speaking, it was also stopping me from breathing. I just stood and looked at her for some time. Not because I was searching for words, but because words wouldn't come out. Finally a deep breath got past the lump.

"Can you put him back in a coma?" I whispered, as my vision began to blur through the wetness. "It was easier then."

Amy's head and shoulders dropped. "I know," she said. "You have to be strong. The next several weeks are going to be difficult. You have to stay strong."

It was becoming painfully clear to me that the better Rick got, the worse I got. That was not true of Mom. As Rick made progress, she made progress. She had been so excited every time I spoke to her over the past week that I expected him to be playing basketball when I saw him next.

Rick was getting better. He was making progress. At the time I didn't realize that my expectations were unrealistic. I couldn't accept the fact that Rick's baby steps were in fact giant steps.

Even when I did realize this in some small way, those steps were becoming more and more painful for me to watch.

Growing up as Rick's little brother, I always looked up to him. I hadn't seen the early steps that Mom helped him make. Now he was taking them again, and once again they were exciting to her. And killing me.

"Thanks, Amy," I said, trying desperately not to come apart in front of her.

20
FINDING HIS WAY

We spent the next few days, starting on February 16, trying to get Rick into the Sticht Center. It seemed that if we weren't fighting with his travel insurance company about moving him back to Canada, we were fighting with his auto policy holder about getting him into the rehab center. And when we weren't fighting with insurance companies, we were downstairs dealing with hospital administration.

The hospital had continued to be very supportive. However, with the travel insurance company balking on the trauma care he had received, administration wanted to be sure they would be paid for his rehab before they agreed to put him into that program. His rehab was the responsibility of his auto policy holder, Wawanessa, which had been excellent to this point. They were proactive and supportive – unlike his travel policy holder who seemed to be focused on nothing but getting out of paying any of their responsibility.

Watching Rick continue his limited rehab in 1105 had not become any easier. I always tried to leave the room without anyone noticing whenever the rehab nurse came in. I knew I was supposed to be excited when he finally figured out that the toothbrush was for his mouth, not his hair. But somehow I just couldn't feel or share it. It wasn't that I didn't want to support Rick in his medical comeback, if that's what it was. It was that I couldn't.

Rick was still on the kick that he was in Mt. Tremblant. Although the hospital staff had been telling us not to worry about it, it was driving me crazy. It became my mission to convince him that we were in North Carolina. The hospital said we could start taking him on day trips. Hell, this was North Carolina so there had to be a NASCAR team somewhere nearby. I looked into it and found that Travis Carter Motorsports was just down the road from the hospital. They ran a team in the NASCAR Winston Cup Series and their driver was Chad Little. I decided to call them.

"Travis Carter Motorsports," a female voice on the other end of the line said.

"Hi, my name is Chris Bye, and I have kind of a strange request," I said.

"Yes, how can I help you?"

"Well, my brother was in a major accident and he is in the North Carolina Baptist Hospital here in Winston-Salem," I started.

"Was he the one on his way to Daytona?" she asked.

"Yeah, sure was. So you heard about it?"

"Yeah, sure did. How can we help?"

"Well, for some reason he thinks he's in Quebec. I know if I was to bring him to your shop he would believe he was in North Carolina. He knows for sure that you guys are not in Quebec. So do you think it would be all right if I brought him over?"

"Sure, no problem. You can bring him over anytime."

Racers, though incredibly competitive, are at the same time incredibly compassionate. A friend of mine once told me that people who are passionate about anything are passionate about life. I think there's some truth to that. I was looking forward to taking Rick out for the first time and I couldn't wait to see his face when we pulled up to Travis Carter's shop. I didn't saying anything to him. He wouldn't have believed me anyhow. I planned to take him on Monday.

– – –

"Hey, did you know they took me for a drive yesterday?" Rick asked that Monday morning.

"No. I saw you yesterday and you never said anything."

"Yeah, I didn't know they were taking me out, but they got us in a van after you left yesterday and took us out to some mall," Rick said, his voice slow and steady.

"So, what, they took you in your wheelchair around the mall?"

"Yep, and you know what was at the mall?"

"No, what?"

"A NASCAR store. You know it's really screwed up. I know that I'm in Mt. Tremblant, but on the other hand I know there's no NASCAR store in Tremblant. Going to the NASCAR store convinced me that I am in North Carolina. But it is really screwed up. I don't know how to explain it. It's like I'm living a waking dream. It's all a fog. I'm having a hard time separating what's real and what's not."

He turned and stared out the window. I knew what he felt like. I have had my share of nights not really knowing where I was. But those nights had nothing to do with hitting my head and everything to do with partying a little too much. It struck me as funny that Rick was probably experiencing for the first time what I had experienced many times, without ever having tasted alcohol.

I did see this as a major step for him. Why his coming to know he was in North Carolina was such a big deal to me I really don't know. There had been so many other steps that had been more significant. He was now recognizing people. He wasn't always right, but he was usually close. He answered the TV remote. Okay, it kind of looks like a cell phone. And he had begun to feed himself. A little messy, but it was a start.

Rick finally got into the Sticht Center, on February 20. Blanche at Wawanessa had pulled some strings to get him in. She never did say for sure, but I think she may have put her job on the line, telling a few little white lies to get him in there. We were very grateful to her and to Wawanessa for this.

The Sticht Center was to have the most profound effect on Rick's quality of life. The North Carolina Baptist Hospital had done its job. They saved his life. Now it was up to the Sticht Center to work their magic.

We spent the next several weeks watching Rick as well as many others get better. One of the rehab nurses came to us one day laughing. At the end of his session one day, she told us, the nurses heard a slamming sound. They left their station to find Rick sitting in his wheelchair pulling on the locked doors of the gym. He told them matter-of-factly that he wanted to go back in and work out some more. They said it was the first time they had ever seen that, because the sessions were grueling.

I was finally beginning to believe that Rick was going to be okay. I don't know why, but I felt a sense of calm. Rick and I had worked so much together in the past. I just knew he would not stop. To this point he hadn't even realized he was sick. Now that he knew he was, he wouldn't stop until he was better. I had seen Rick set his eye on goals in the past, goals that everyone said were unattainable. And I couldn't remember him failing to reach any of them.

True, he still believed the girl on TV had just been in his room. That he had fish living in his knee. That the TV clicker was a cell phone. But now he also believed that he was sick and that he needed to work to get better.

Connie had called to say she was coming down to see him again. We still didn't understand Rick's relationship with her. She didn't seem like his type. And she had kids, which made no sense whatsoever. Rick never liked kids. Or maybe he did. I had to admit I didn't know because we had never talked about it. Pretty much the only thing Rick and I ever talked about were cars: Porsches, in particular, and race cars.

21
LEAVING HOME

The next several weeks, moving on into March, were chock full of triumphs and challenges. Rick had a long way to go but continued to show great progress. It was obvious the rehab was working.

The phone calls from friends and family began to shift in tone and content. People were asking what Rick was going to do when he got back. Did I think he would race again?

We had started to make arrangements to come home. Rick would have to leave Winston-Salem in a wheelchair. At first that was a little difficult for us to deal with. The rest of the family and I hoped Rick would be able to walk out of the hospital. But the fact that he was going to leave the hospital in anything other than a box was amazing. We decided that Rick, Mom, and I would fly home together.

We arranged that we would fly from Greensboro to Buffalo. From there we would drive home to St. Catharines. We booked ourselves into first class because the seats were bigger and Rick would be much more comfortable.

It wasn't going to be easy leaving the friends we had made at the hospital and rehab center. In fact, everyone we had met in Winston-Salem had become family. There was something truly special about the people who touched our lives there. They may have been the most genuine and sincere of anyone I had met during twenty or so years of traveling. Southern hospitality is not a myth. When people asked you how you were, whether in a restaurant, a hotel, a video store or even just out on the street, they truly meant it.

I thought about a very different experience just up the seaboard in New Jersey. How could people who lived so close to each other be so different?

We were working at the Meadowlands up there doing a launch for Mercedes Benz. The Meadowlands is a great facility for training drivers. The parking lot is big enough to host an Indy Car race, which they did in the late 1980s.

Don't get me wrong, I like the people of New Jersey. They just have a very different way of showing their hospitality than southeners.

Hank, Bob, and I went into a restaurant for lunch one day a couple of miles from the Meadowlands. The place wasn't that busy, yet we stood at the door for quite a long time before anyone came to seat us. Hank is without a doubt the single most impatient person in the world. He gets impatient at red lights, at McDonald's, and especially at the bank. When a teller turns their sign around to the "Next Teller" side, Hank doesn't wait until the next teller is available, like most people. He simply walks up to the wicket, turns the sign around, and hands the teller what he wants to deposit or withdraw.

Hank was huffing and puffing. Finally a girl came over to us, grabbed three menus, and walked away without saying a word. We all looked at each other, shrugged, and followed her. Boy, was Hank pissed. The waitress led us to a table by the window and turned and walked away as if we didn't exist.

We sat and talked about work as we watched the endless stream of corporate jets taking off and landing. We were within a mile or two of Teeterborough International Airport, which must be one of the busiest corporate airports in the US. We were so caught up in the air show, it took us awhile before we realized that no one had come by to get our order.

"Excuse me, could we get some drinks?" I asked someone who looked like she worked there.

"I'm busy," this young girl said in a deep raspy voice without so much as a look in our direction.

"Alrighty then," I said. Hank and Bob looked at each other in disbelief.

"Come on, let's get the hell out of here," Hank said with a scowl. Hank could get his face so long it would take scaffolding to hold it up.

"Hank, I've been here for a while and all the restaurants are the same," I said.

Hank gave me a look that would frighten Charles Manson. Bob and I looked at each other and started to laugh.

"Excuse me, do you work here?" Hank said to a young lady in a striped uniform.

"Yep," she replied and walked away without skipping a beat. Bob and I almost fell off our chairs laughing. Hank just sat there in shock.

After we got some service and food, we didn't dare ask for ketchup.

– – –

Part of me wanted to go home and get back to work, and part of me wanted to stay in Winston-Salem. I know it may seem odd, but my desire to stay was stronger than my desire to leave.

I thought about the words I would use when we finally said goodbye to everyone at the center and hospital. I rehearsed them a hundred times over. I knew, however, that the words were unlikely to come out the way I hoped. There was a good chance they wouldn't come out at all.

I thought about all of the people I was going to miss. There were many, but I was going to miss Amy Olson the most. She had brought me comfort exactly when I needed it most. If I was a religious person I'd say she was an angel. She always appeared at the most trying times. She was suddenly there when I was out in the hall trying to catch my breath after Rick didn't know who I was. She would walk past us in the ICU as if unaware of us and then offer a slight grin. Amy had very little to say, but what she did say mattered.

I was going to miss Mike Chang, the trauma team leader. I will never forget meeting him for the first time when he led the medical team to Rick's bedside in the ICU. There we were – Cathy, my parents, and I – shocked, confused, and afraid. Mike was cautiously optimistic and full of confidence. We all liked him from the moment we met him.

The thing I remember most from that very first conversation was when Dr. Chang said that Rick was very sick. Sick, I thought. He ain't sick. He's fucked up. Sick is when you have a cold.

Laurel in administration had been nothing short of spectacular to deal with, putting us at ease about paying the hospital bills from the very beginning of our ordeal.

All of the nurses in the ICU would be missed as much as the doctors. Every single one was compassionate and professional.

I was going to miss the rehab therapists, too, how they worked without drawing attention to themselves.

We were leaving this place in debt. We had been asked to sign a personal guarantee saying that if Rick's insurance company refused to pay, we would. That debt would be easy to repay. We figured we could sell our house.

But there were several other debts that we could never repay, debts that will go unpaid till the day we die. We could never repay the people who removed Rick from the burning wreckage. Or the ones who air-lifted him to the hospital. We couldn't repay the people who worked in the ER, or the trauma team who worked on him in the OR. We couldn't repay the nurses from ICU 5B, or the rehab therapists, or the entire hospital staff.

As I sat beside Rick the day before leaving the hospital, it was clear that he was becoming more and more aware of his surroundings. He still wasn't making perfect sense when he opened his mouth, but he was making great progress. When he wasn't working on his rehab, he spent a lot of time just lying around, looking and talking. There were spells when you couldn't shut him up and others when he wouldn't say a word.

"Hey, do you remember the time that 928 got stuck in the ditch at Westwood?" I asked him, partly to pass the time and partly to see what his memory was like.

Rick grinned and I knew that he knew exactly what I was talking about.

We were at Westwood Racetrack outside Vancouver for another Porsche Advanced Driving School. It was 1988. As usual it was raining when we arrived.

It was early in the weekend and we had just started our first lapping session, the time when students get to drive the track for the first time after a series of exercises. The head of the Porsche division of Volkswagen Canada at the time, Michael Ney, was a good friend to all of us. He always wanted to be part of the crowd and every once in a while insisted on acting as an instructor. We were always happy to have him help. Michael had been to many track events and was actually a pretty good driver, but he didn't have the experience or credentials of the instructors.

Michael was given a young Asian guy to instruct who had just bought a brand new 928S. I always liked the 928, but the car took a lot of flack from most Porsche enthusiasts. For a big, heavy car, it handled exceptionally well.

Michael and his student were about halfway through their lapping session and things were going pretty well. But while they were exiting the long right-hand corner that leads onto the back straight, the rear end of the 928 started to slide. Most instructors would very calmly add a little throttle input with slight counter steer and everything would be all right. Well, Michael and his student didn't do that. I don't know what they did, but when I got to the scene, the 928 was firmly planted in a ditch on the driver's right. That's race talk for the right side of the road – if you are pointed in the right direction when you finally stop, that is.

The shiny new 928 was up to its door handles in grass and mud, and Michael and his student were standing beside the car looking confused. Hank and a couple of the other guys had stopped and we started to talk about how we were going to get the car out of the ditch. It wasn't going to be easy. The car was wedged in the ditch lengthwise.

As we stood on the track in the rain, a crowd gathered. Nobody had to ask who had been in the car. Michael and his student's guilty looks said it all. Someone finally suggested we get one of the rental cars and place it behind the Porsche then hook up a rope between the two and pull the Porsche out.

Michael volunteered his rental. We guided him as he pulled up behind the Porsche. The ditch ended so we were able to place the rental car fairly close to the Porsche. As we got the car close, someone went under the rear of the Porsche and found a safe place to hook up the tow rope. Then they went under the front of the rental car and attached the other end of the rope.

So there the two cars sat, nose to tail, one stuck and one not. Michael, getting into the rental car, instructed his student to take the driver's seat in the Porsche. The way Michael had explained it, the guy in the 928 was going to put his car in reverse while he would do the same in the rental car. Together they would become unstuck. Seeing that Michael was the boss of Porsche Canada, we all just stood back and let him take control.

"Okay," Michael yelled from his car. "I am going to back up and get tension on the tow rope. Once there is tension, I'll get on the gas. You make sure your car is in reverse and you stand on the gas as well. Okay?"

The owner of the 928 nodded – no smile, no "okay," just a fast up-and-down nod that told us that he hadn't understood a word. He sat in his Porsche with the driver's door open and the gear lever in reverse, looking intently over his left shoulder, waiting for Michael's lead to jump on the gas.

Michael had his car in reverse and was backing up slowly, just enough to take up the slack in the tow rope. As the rope went tight, Michael looked first to us, then to the entire instructor roster standing in the rain not quite sure what they were about to witness, and then to his student – his customer – and nodded. The proud young owner of the 928 nodded back.

Michael turned his head over his right shoulder and slowly, but firmly, started putting pressure on the throttle. His car was having trouble getting a grip in the wet grass, so he did what any of us would have done: apply more throttle. But there were four things that none of us had thought of. First, the rental car was front-wheel drive. Second, it was parked behind the Porsche. Third, it was in reverse. And fourth, the driver's door of the Porsche was open.

When Michael stood on the gas, the perfect threesome of rainwater, grass, and mud emerged from the bottom of the rental car's front tires and headed straight toward the Porsche's open door at about a thousand miles an hour. None of us will ever forget the look on the Porsche owner's face, a look that actually disappeared under a cone of mud, water, and grass. Just as the young man was walloped in the face, his hand slipped off the door handle. He scrambled to reach for the door to get it closed. Michael, meanwhile, began turning the steering wheel one way then the other with the throttle still firmly planted on the floor, searching for grip, all the while looking behind him.

The wedge of grass and mud continued to fly and the Porsche owner continued to reach unsuccessfully for the door. The pile of shit just kept inching higher and higher on the dash of the Porsche. We couldn't see any gauges or lights. Just grass, mud, and more grass.

What were we to do? Here was our leader not only plastering this poor bastard with grass and mud but also adding hundreds of pounds to the gross weight of his Porsche. If we had been responsible, dedicated staff members, we would have tried to get Michael's attention to get him to stop. But we were not. It only took one of us to look at another of us and we all started laughing our asses off. We were on our knees on the track with tears of laughter streaming down our faces. Hank's reaction was priceless. He looked like he was in shock. He didn't know what the hell to do. He seemed to be weighing his options:

1. Try to help the poor bastard getting bombarded in the Porsche.

2. Try to stop Michael from bombarding the poor bastard in the Porsche.

3. Kill all of us for not making the situation any better.

Hank chose none of the above. He just stood there and kept staring.

Finally Michael decided he should take a look and see how things were going. He slowly lifted his foot off the gas and turned to see if the Porsche had moved.

The look on Michael's face is as clear to me today as it was all those years ago. It was total shock.

Of course, we all found the look on his face absolutely hilarious. Those of us standing were now back down on the track crying.

As we all tried to catch our breath we knew we shouldn't be laughing – the poor bastard in the car could have been hit by a rock or something. Hell, he could have drowned. As I looked at Michael I saw his shocked expression change, not for better or worse, just change. I think maybe it was his eyes that just got a little bigger that made me look back toward the Porsche.

Sasquatch.

Sasquatch was climbing out of the Porsche.

The poor bastard was covered from head to toe with green slime and mud. He was trying to claw the mud from his eye sockets as he stood there. I was laughing so hard I couldn't catch my breath. My stomach was killing me. Even Hank couldn't hold back any longer. As Sasquatch turned to check out the condition of his new car, we took the hilarity up a notch. We knew it was probably time to stop laughing, but we couldn't.

Hell, I'm sure there's grass in that car to this day. The sad thing was that the poor owner of the Porsche never did find the incident funny. I guess he just didn't get our brand of humor.

— — —

The late March morning dew was almost dry as Mom and I walked out of the Hawthorne. I looked up at the hotel for the last time as we prepared to make the final trip to the hospital. Rick was coming home.

We found Rick sitting in his wheelchair beside his bed, folding his clothes. He looked a hundred years old.

"I don't think I can carry all this shit," he said as he looked around the room. "It really is amazing just how much stuff you can collect when you're in the hospital for a couple of months."

"Yeah, well I'm sure the nurses will take care of anything we can't carry," I said.

I sat in the corner and let Rick put his stuff together. I wanted to help but knew that would be intruding. Mom realized this, too. This was his stuff. This was his room. I remembered one of the conversations I had with Amy Olson early on. She told me not to worry because Rick wouldn't remember any of this.

Rick had asked the doctors what would happen next time he hit his head. Their reply was, "The only thing we know for sure is that it won't be good." His doctors had been evasive about what they thought his level of recovery would be. If they told us once they told us a hundred times that we would simply have to wait and see. They were confident as far as his broken bones were concerned. They just didn't know where he would end up as far as his head injury was concerned. They were always optimistic, but their cautiousness was always evident.

I knew he wouldn't remember leaving Winston-Salem. It's true he finally knew that's where he was. But he hadn't even experienced the city.

Much as I didn't want to leave, I knew I needed to get back to work. I had effectively shut my life down for the past two months. Hank had been carrying the load and he needed me back.

"I think I've got everything," Rick said as he closed his bag on the bed.

"Okay, well, let's go then," I said with a lump in my throat.

As we walked out of Rick's room, we saw a huge lineup of people waiting for us. I don't know how many nurses were there but it seemed like dozens. There were nurses from ICU 5B, the eleventh floor, and of course the Sticht Center. Standing at the end of the line were Dr. Michael Chang and Dr. Amy Olson. I was so happy they had taken the time to come over to the rehab center to see us off.

I pushed Rick down the line in his wheelchair and everyone was shaking hands and hugging. It was truly a very emotional time. When we got to the end of the line, I looked at Dr. Chang and Dr. Olson. My eyes were going to have to do all the communicating. I just didn't know what to say.

"It doesn't work like this," I heard Amy saying as we approached her. She looked at me and expanded on her comment. "He has no right to be leaving this place," she said quietly. "He has no right to be leaving this place."

My eyes began to well up.

"He is a very lucky boy," she said.

"Thank you," I said as my chin began to quiver. I wanted to say so much more, but words seemed so hollow. I hoped everyone there knew just how much they had done for our family. I turned as the elevator door closed and saw everyone standing there smiling and waving.

I pushed Rick through the lobby of the hospital and into the parking garage. It was cold outside. And quiet. *Click, click, click,* our heels echoed in the parking garage. It was the same sound I remembered hearing when we arrived two months ago, only without the *besheeeh.*

"Wow, that's pretty good," I said to Rick as he pulled himself out of his wheelchair and into the passenger seat of the rental car. "You been practicing?"

"Yep," he said proudly.

The hospital faded in the mirror as we pulled out of the parkade and turned the car toward the Greensboro airport.

"How far did you say the airport was?" Rick asked.

"About forty-five minutes."

Rick, Mom, and I drove the rest of the way to the airport without saying a word.

– – –

As we sat at the gate waiting for our flight to arrive I started to wonder just how the hell you got a wheelchair down the aisle of a plane. I figured the airline staff would help. I got up and pushed Rick up to the gate to prepare for pre-board. I had been on probably a thousand airplanes in my life and this was the first time I ever pre-boarded.

We settled into our third-row business-class seats. Wawanessa was continuing to take care of the flights. They were very understanding when I asked about flying up front. They were agreeable when I explained that it would be almost impossible for Rick to fly in coach. His legs still weren't one hundred percent and if anyone bumped him it could cause major problems.

Before we knew it, the flight was over. As the captain prepared the cabin for landing in Buffalo, Rick leaned over to me and said, "I want to stop and see the guys at Bicknell's before we get home."

"No problem," I said.

– – –

Bicknell's was Bicknell Race Products, on the east side of St. Catharines. Pete Bicknell is from St. Catharines and the premier builder of dirt stock cars in North America. The cars he builds are called Dirt Modifies. Rick spent a few years racing dirt cars at the local dirt tracks. The track in St. Catharines is Merrittville Speedway. It is a third of a mile banked dirt oval. Back when Rick was driving, the cars were crude but fast. Rick used to say that they were like a five hundred horsepower John Deere tractor.

Cathy was happy when Rick decided to pack in his dirt career because she knew it meant I wouldn't be asking her to go to the dirt tracks around home and in upstate New York. She hated those tracks, and for good reason. They were dirty and loud and we would always stay until late into the night having a few beers after the races.

There was one night, in particular, that she will never forget or forgive me for.

We were going out to meet some friends for dinner on a Friday night but I insisted on going first to Ransomville Speedway just outside Lewiston, New York, to watch Rick race. Ransomville is a half-mile track and fast as hell. Since we were going out after, we were definitely not dressed for the dirt track. Dirt track attire is blue jeans and nothing better. We arrived at Ransomville late, as usual, and had to park about a half mile from the gate and walk through the muddy parking lot. It had rained much of the week.

About the only vacant seats were right at the bottom at the exit of turn 4. In fact, there was practically no one sitting there.

WAAAAAAAAAAAA, the bombers all screamed together as every one of the drivers slammed the throttle to the ground trying their best to get to corner 1 first. The bomber class of cars is the entry level of dirt cars. They are the cheapest cars to run, and they look like it. They kind of look like a beat up street car. The field moved into corner 1 in two trains, like snakes sliding in sequence. The leader was approaching corner 3 and there was a huge cloud of dust rising on the back straight. I looked over at Cath. I knew what she was thinking. Something like: "I just can't wait for that cloud of dust to get over here to the grandstands and fill my hair, my nose, and my teeth with dirt."

As the leader slid out of corner 3 and directly into corner 4 it looked like he was carrying a little too much speed. His car slowly left the low groove on the inside of the track and started to plow right toward where we were sitting. His chicken wire grill was coming straight at us. No big deal – there was a steel guardrail and big concrete blocks between the track and the grandstands.

On the other side of the steel guardrail and cement blocks, which we were sitting right behind, was a very large and very deep ditch and it was full of rainwater. The problem was that the bomber had disappeared into it. Judging by the size of the wave the car was creating, the ditch was also full of dark, slimy clay mud.

BAM. The bomber hit the concrete. The tsunami of muck that was about to cover us was at least fifteen feet high. We slowly turned our heads toward each other, as I covered the top of my Bud with one hand. We knew it would be fruitless to try to get out of the way.

WHAM. The great wave hit the lower section of the grandstand. I put my index fingers into my eye sockets and tried to clean out the chunks before attempting to open my eyes. What did I see but Cathy covered from head to toe in this slimy cocktail. This was not a happy woman beside me. I took a long pull on my beer. Ummmm, good. I looked back at her. I couldn't help it. I started laughing my head off. She started to grin. She was pissed, but she had to admit it was pretty damn funny. There we were, two of only a few morons who knew nothing about the secret lake. The entire grandstands were killing themselves laughing.

Cathy proceeded to the ladies room to salvage whatever was left of her going-out look. I'm pretty sure that was the last time she ever went to a dirt track.

— — —

After we landed at Buffalo International Airport we got into my car and headed for the border.

"How long away?" the Canadian Immigration officer asked.

"Oh, about two months," I replied.

"Did you buy or receive anything?"

"Well I didn't, but he received a shattered left pelvis, a subdural hematoma, a contusion on the right side of his brain, a nearly severed right foot, and, oh yeah, a hole drilled in his head." I looked over at Rick. "Anything else?"

"Nope, I think that's about it."

The officer leaned down and looked over at Rick and smiled. "Any alcohol or cigarettes?" he asked.

"Nope, that stuff is bad for you," I said as I slowly drove away from the booth.

"We're here," I said as I turned off Cushman Road and into Bicknell Racing Products.

We parked and I helped Rick into his wheelchair. As I rolled him up to the door, we were met by Larry, Pete, Randy, and all the guys. It was good to be home and really good to see some familiar faces.

It wasn't as if Rick and I were really close to any of these guys, but racers are racers and always enjoy being together.

Rick started to tell the guys that he was doing just fine and that he was right back to normal. He went on and on and on. It was important to him to make sure everyone knew he was okay. About an hour later we took our leave and headed home.

For the next while, home for Rick would be our parents' house. Wawanessa had paid to have a wheelchair lift installed on the front porch.

The next several weeks would see a steady flow of visitors to our parents' home. It felt like Grand Central Station. The very first weekend home Rick must have had a hundred visitors along with his girlfriend, Connie, and her kids. Cathy and I had agreed to take Connie's kids to our place for the weekend to give my parents a break. It had been over two months now and Mom had not left Rick's side. She and Dad used to say that once you have a child, that child is yours forever, whether five or fifty. I guess they're right.

22
A NIGHT TO
REMEMBER

I t didn't take long before all of us realized we were going to have to pitch in to help Rick out with his bills. But Rick wasn't the only one who needed help. Cathy and I were the ones who had signed a personal guarantee to get him out of the hospital. I wonder what they would have done if we had not signed it. Keep him as ransom and charge us storage?

We still had no idea of the intentions of the travel insurance company. It seemed that up to this point they had done everything possible to get out of paying. We had no reason to believe that this attitude was going to change.

I'm not really sure how the topic came up, but somehow we began to discuss the idea of having a fundraiser. We talked about having a Motorsport Gala evening. With all of the concerned people who called while we were in North Carolina, we were pretty sure we would have a good turnout. We put the wheels in motion for what would become one of the most memorable evenings in Canadian motorsport history, the Rick Bye Benefit Dinner.

We chose the Sheraton Hotel and Conference Centre in Markham, just north of Toronto. They told us that they could seat 300 people. At $150 a head, getting that many out would be great.

Porsche really stepped up to the plate, helping us organize the dinner. With much assistance from the company's Susan Marsili, we assembled a great group of people to plan and direct the evening. Bob Carlson, also from Porsche, agreed to bring a couple of the Porsche museum cars for display. With all the Porsche enthusiasts that Rick knew, having these cars there would ensure a large crowd.

The level of support offered to our family continued to humble us. There was an endless stream of phone calls from people who wanted to help with the event. I think it was largely because the people who knew us knew we didn't really have any money. It's easy for people to assume that racers have a lot of money since they know how expensive racing is. That couldn't have been further from the truth for Rick and me.

Most people, including Rick himself, and me, for that matter, couldn't figure out where Rick got the money to race at the levels that he had. He just had this burning desire that wouldn't allow him to quit.

With the help of Porsche Cars North America and the Porsche Club of America, Upper Canada Region, the $150 tickets were flying out the door. We set a date of Saturday, May 2, 1998, for the event.

Canadian automobile journalist Jim Kenzie had come up with the idea of holding a silent auction as part of the evening. We started canvassing various people for donations of things to bid on. With ticket sales moving at a blistering pace, we approached the hotel to see if we could get any more people into the room. Fortunately, they could seat an additional fifty people. It wouldn't take long for those extra tickets to be spoken for.

Our entire family agreed very early on that it was only fair for us to pay for our own tickets. We really didn't know where the money raised was going to go, but there was no doubt that it would be put to good use.

Several companies bought tables, including Porsche, Jaguar, Mazda, and Performance Cars from St. Catharines, to name a few. Rick wasn't one to say much, but you could tell he was truly touched by the outpouring of support.

As the night approached, we all worked very hard to put the final details in place. There were cars to get to the hotel for display, an overflow of ticket requests, and an endless stream of phone calls from just about everywhere. Pretty much everyone from the motorsport community who had not bought tickets were now calling and trying to get in. There were also many who called and said they wouldn't be able to make it, but who wanted to support us by donating the amount of the ticket.

The evening was emceed by Jim Kenzie and Canadian racing legend Bill Adam. Jim and Bill got the evening started with a bang. The chemistry between them was special and one they shared with everyone in the room. The guest speakers included sports car racing legend Hurley Haywood and Canadian Indy star Scott Goodyear. Stu Ballentyne from Molstar Entertainment also had some very touching words, ending with, "Thank God for Rick Bye."

Next up was Hurley. He spoke about some of his racing days but then quickly got onto the subject of Rick.

Rick was sitting at the head table with the rest of the family along with his girlfriend, Connie. He was very quiet most of the evening. As people spoke he sat quietly, humbled, his head hung low looking up at the speakers only when he found the strength. I'm sure he didn't want to break down in front of this large group of people. I, on the other hand, was focused on preparing for my turn to speak so I didn't really focus too much on Rick. I also knew that every person in the room had their eyes on him as he sat and listened to the individuals who had so graciously joined us that night. Some of these people made their living as guest speakers making thousands of dollars per speech. This night no one got five cents. They all did it for Rick and for our family. We were all very moved by this fact.

Hurley said there were many times when he and Rick worked together that Rick would say something and Hurley would just look at him. Then a couple of hours later he would start laughing. Rick had a razor sharp sense of humor. I wondered during all of this if it would ever come back.

After Hurley came Scott Goodyear. He was, without a doubt, the person who most deserved to win the Indy 500. Scott finished second twice, once to Al Unser Jr. in the closest finish in the history of the race. What many had forgotten was the fact that Scott started last and finished second by a couple thousandths of a second. Scott was a Formula Atlantic Champion and the motorsport press called him the

Ice Man. He is a driver who never really looks fast but always is. No matter what Scott drove, he was a threat to win the race. He and Rick had raced against each other in the Rothmans Porsche Turbo Cup Series.

In his speech, Scott told the story of crashing his Indy Car in Brazil and breaking his back. He said he didn't want to be operated on in Brazil. In fact, he didn't want anyone other than Indy Car surgeon Dr. Terry Trammel to see him. There were no immediate scheduled flights to the US at that time, so Scott agreed to be strapped to a pallet and be placed in the back of a FedEx cargo jet. He was promptly couriered to Miami with a 10 a.m. or free guarantee. From Miami, he was taken up to Indianapolis, where Dr. Trammel worked his magic on his back.

I was up next. I realized that all of the other speakers did just that for a living, speak. And I didn't. I wasn't really nervous, though, because I had been so busy in the weeks leading up to the gala. I had spent some time putting a speech together, not that I planned to follow it word for word. I just needed some reminders. My biggest fear was forgetting to thank one of the so many people who had helped us. There was no doubt that I knew the story, so talking about it shouldn't be a problem.

I had read somewhere that the best way to kick off a speech was to get people laughing. I figured if the experts said it worked, then it must. After thanking Jim, Bill, and the other speakers, I began: "I have prepared a speech and have been practicing for several weeks. And one thing that I have realized is that speeches are much like sex. It always goes perfect when you're alone."

That got a laugh, and I continued, now more relaxed.

"I know that most of you know Rick and that the only thing he has ever drunk stronger than Diet Coke is regular Coke. But that hasn't always been the case. When we were kids Rick had a serious drug problem. He used to experiment with psychedelic drugs. Yeah, it's true, it was a real problem. He used to take handfuls of different-colored pills and cram them down my throat just to see what would happen."

That worked, too. Everyone was getting a kick out of my speech so far, but the hard part was to come.

"There was a time not that long ago when I thought that we would all be meeting under very different circumstances. I pictured all of us here now standing around a hole in the ground somewhere, freezing our asses off. I have to tell you that the support that you, the motorsport community, have shown our family has been nothing short of amazing. In fact, your support has been, at times, very hard to listen to. It was hard to hear so many people hurting.

"I knew Rick had a lot of friends, but I had no idea just how many. Listening to literally hundreds of unfinished messages on our voicemail was difficult. I can't tell you how many of you left messages that started with, 'Hi, this is so and so ... I have known Rick for some time through the Porsche Club or racing or wherever. Would you please tell Rick that I called and ...' And then, *click*.

"We all knew that you weren't being rude. We knew you hung up because the words you were looking for wouldn't come out. I knew all about the lump that grew in your throat, because it was the same lump that grew in mine.

"Whether it was Vic Sifton, who talked his way to the side of the road as he left a message because he was having a hard time seeing through his tears, or whether it was Big Ernst, who seized up after getting out, 'Hi Chris, it's Ernst,' pause, short hard breath ... *click*, we knew then, we know now, and we thank you."

I went on to thank all of the people who helped with the night and all of the companies who had bought tables. I thanked everyone and every company on my list, looking to Cathy to see if I had forgotten anyone. During my time on stage I knew I could not look at Rick, or anyone else at our table for that matter. I did catch the odd glimpse of Rick. He had his head down with his chin on his chest. I knew he also could not look at me.

It was now time to introduce Rick. He had been getting around in a wheelchair for the most part. But this night he had insisted on walking in. It was important to him that people who had not seen him since the accident saw him walking. During the cocktail reception before dinner, everyone was standing around talking and laughing with people they had not seen for some time. I'm not sure how long I had been standing there when a strange and sudden calm came over the room. I looked up and saw that everyone was looking in the direction of the entrance. I knew Rick had just made his way down the hall. I'm sure that many who had not seen him since before the accident were a little shocked. He had put some weight back on since leaving the hospital but still wasn't anywhere near the weight he was before. He was gaunt – and frail.

But to much amazement – mostly from me, I'm sure – there he was, a cane in each hand, each step coming slowly, cautiously, and painfully. He looked up and smiled. Or perhaps it was more of a grimace, trying to hide the pain. Just three months earlier he was lying in a hospital bed with his legs and feet smashed like oatmeal. Putting even his light weight on them must have hurt like hell.

When Rick was called to the stage, it took all his strength to slide his chair back from the table, gather his canes, and begin the slow and painful task of standing. He was still very unsteady on his feet and his biggest fear was falling. Not because of the damage and pain he would cause himself but because of the humiliation of falling in front of his peers. With every eye in the room on him, he took one deliberate step after the other. His gaze was straight and focused. He made it to the podium. There was relief in his face.

Rick started off by thanking everyone and he was obviously overwhelmed as were we with the response from the motorsport community and friends.

Rick struggled a little finding the words he was looking for. The evening must have seemed a little strange because he didn't remember much, if anything, of North Carolina. The only thing he knew of the support everyone gave him while he was down there was what he had been told. It was obvious, however, that he did know of the support the community was showing him, and us, that night. And that was very humbling to him. He kept his head down as he thanked everyone, never once looking up from the podium. I'm sure he was afraid of breaking down if he did look up. And I'm sure that simply standing in one spot hurt like hell.

Everyone was touched, and relieved to see and finally hear his voice. They all knew he still had a long and painful road ahead of him. But they also knew that the road would be one traveled, not lost.

As I walked back to my seat I looked over the crowd and was over-come. I think it was at that moment that I realized, for the first time, that there were hundreds of people in the room. People who were there to support our family. They weren't there to say, "Hey, look at me." They were there for one reason, to support Rick and the rest of us.

Now that my time on stage was over, I wasted no time in getting to the bar. I hadn't had a drink all night and Lord knew I was ready for one or two.

23
THE RACE
OF OUR LIVES

O n August 20, 1998, Joanne, head of finance of the
North Carolina Baptist Hospital, called me on my cell phone to
inform me that the insurance company had denied our claim in full.
She told me I needed to make arrangements to get her a check for
$128,000 US. As I was speaking to her, a call came in on my other
line and I told her I would call her right back because I had to take
a call I was waiting for.

"Chris Bye," I said as I answered the phone.

"Oh, hi Chris, this is Suzanne from Rick's insurance company."
This was not the call I was waiting for after all.

"Well, your timing is impeccable."

"Oh, so this is a good time then?"

"I just hung up from the North Carolina Baptist Hospital who
told me you have denied our claim in its entirety."

"Well, Chris, that's why I'm calling," Suzanne said in a sweet
southern accent. "You see, we don't even have a file on your
brother's case. There seems to be nothing whatsoever here."

"Oh, really, so are you calling to ask me out for dinner?"

There was a long pause.

"Suzanne, are you calling to ask me out for dinner?"

"Uh, what do you mean?"

"Well, I didn't call you. You called me and if you're telling me that you have no file on us, then why are you calling, and where did you get my number?"

Silence.

"Suzanne, there's a movie starring your company. It's called *The Rainmaker*. It's based on a John Grisham book. Have you seen it?"

Silence.

"Suzanne, let me tell you something. We have support from a few companies where you would be nothing more than another file on the desk of one of their lawyers. If you want to have a very loud, public, dragged-through-the-mud lawsuit, then let's get on with it. Suzanne, you sound like a nice girl. How do you sleep at night? You and your company have put our family through hell. You don't give a shit about anything other than not paying out. That's the only thing you focus on, how you can screw the little guy. Well, Suzanne, listen very carefully. Don't call me or any member of my family again. You write *do not call* on that file of ours that doesn't exist. Have I made myself perfectly clear?"

"Mr. Bye, you don't –"

"Goodbye, Suzanne."

Seven days later the North Carolina Baptist Hospital received a check paying off the balance of our account. The insurance company had met their commitment. Only because they felt they had no choice. In hindsight I guess I shouldn't be surprised that they didn't want to pay. Perhaps that's what one should expect from an insurance company.

– – –

It was years before I began to understand why I was falling apart as Rick was slowly getting better. Publicly I stood tall. Privately, I would self-destruct. As the days turned into nights, and the nights into weeks, and the weeks into months, my armor slowly started to crack.

My life, thus far, had been simple. I was selfish and self-centered and did what I wanted, when I wanted. Throughout this ordeal, I learned a lesson – a difficult but valuable one – that changed me forever.

The teacher of this lesson followed me and never left my side.

At times, I wanted so badly for this teacher to just piss off, but no. The teacher shadowed me from the time I got out of bed in the morning till the time I fell back asleep. Even with my eyes closed, the teacher was there. He would reach into my chest and squeeze my heart so hard the pain would make my knees weak. Weak to the point where they would just give out and I would lean against a wall and crumble into a weak, lame, pathetic mess. It would have been so much easier to just stay there against the wall, on the floor, and give up. But it was that teacher – a teacher I call *tenacity* – who made me get up.

Rick and I had both been selfish. Rick had allowed racing to take precedence over good things in his life – women who had supported him through thick and thin. That didn't matter, though. As soon as there was a crack in their armor, he headed for the hills.

I, on the other hand, was different. I was also unbelievably selfish, but I was not willing to let Cathy go. Or maybe she just didn't leave. Lord knows I gave her more than enough reasons.

It wasn't just racing, though. I was selfish in so many other ways.

If I wanted to go riding my bike with the boys, I went.

If I wanted to go racing, I did.

If I didn't want to go into the delivery room, I didn't.

If I didn't want to change diapers, I didn't.

My life had been pretty simple: decide what I wanted to do, and do it. At any cost.

All the while, Cathy just hung in there. I, and many of our friends, often asked why. I think back to all the races she came to, sleeping in our old makeshift motor home. I think of all the times she sat at home alone while I was off doing my own thing. I think about how I never wanted kids and she did. Hailey is now my best friend and the apple of my eye. I love her so much, more than I ever knew possible.

I had never given much thought about what anyone would think. Maybe this attitude had come from what my mother had told me so many years ago. Who knows?

What I did know, now anyway, was that it was the tenacity that Rick had taught me that ultimately helped me help him. While it almost destroyed me, I learned the true meaning of the word, not only because of his accident, but because of his spirit. I saw tenacity in its purest form, from the doctors to the nurses to the rehab therapists.

But most of all, I saw it in Rick. I now know, if I ever doubted it, that the circumstances of whatever race he was in didn't matter in comparison with one thing: the finish line. If he knew where that was, then that's where he was going to go, and the faster the better.

– – –

Today Rick lives in Mississauga, Ontario, with his wife, Karina. He got married – imagine that. He continues his long relationship with Porsche, managing their press-car fleet in Eastern Canada. He has competed in a few Porsche Club races and continues to look into doing some more racing. His injuries have healed and much of our experience together during his early days of recovery continues to be a mystery to him. The doctors had told us that he would not remember any of what went on at the hospital, and they were right. Rick and I still share the strong bond that motorsport strengthened between us.

I continue to live in St. Catharines with my wife, Cathy, and daughter, Hailey. I continue to work with Franczak and the amazing team of people there. I get to spend my working days with cool cars and cool car people. And my off time with Cathy and Hailey, family and friends. People who make me laugh and thankful for life.